# TEN YEARS ON

# TEN YEARS ON

## BRITAIN WITHOUT THE EUROPEAN UNION

DR LEE ROTHERHAM

FOREWORD BY TREVOR KAVANAGH
EPILOGUE BY FREDERICK FORSYTH

The TaxPayers' Alliance

First published in Great Britain by the TaxPayers' Alliance 2009

ISBN 978–0–95639–200–8

Typeset in Bembo by
RefineCatch Limited, Bungay, Suffolk
Printed and bound in Great Britain by Clays Ltd, St Ives plc

The TaxPayers' Alliance
83 Victoria Street
London SW1H 0HW
www.taxpayersalliance.com
0845 330 9554

*Half way along our life's path,*
*I found myself in a dark wood,*
*For I had lost the road that was true.*
Dante, *Inferno*

# Contents

# Acknowledgements

The very existence of this book is predominantly due to the drive of one man; Julian Blackwell, whose energy and enthusiasm impelled this project along at breakneck speed. Thanks also need to go to Frederick Forsyth CBE and Trevor Kavanagh, two of the most insightful and accessible commentators in print today, for agreeing to pen powerful critiques to put this book into context. Credit is deservedly due to Alan Hamilton for converting key elements of the text for abridged publication and for editing. Finally, thanks to the TPA family for their input into this work and the broader project: Jayne Adye, Katherine Andrew, Lord Blackwell, Matthew Elliott, Ruth Lea, Ian Milne, Kathryn Paul, Sara Rainwater, Matt Sinclair and Mark Wallace.

# Acknowledgements

# Foreword

*by Trevor Kavanagh*

The next election will be fought over cuts in state spending, with all parties searching for big savings without losing core voters.

Yet none is talking about the biggest saving of all – tens of billions of pounds – with the approval of the overwhelming majority of British voters.

This is the cost of our membership of the European Union – soon to be the United States of Europe.

But as Lee Rotherham argues in his glimpse of a possible future, it also includes the cost to our democracy – and the value of our surrendered national sovereignty.

A recent opinion poll shows seven out of ten United Kingdom adults urgently want a say on Britain's continued role as one of 27 member states ruled from Brussels.

They want the chance, promised to them by all three major parties and treacherously repudiated by Labour, of a referendum on the European Constitution which now masquerades as the Lisbon Treaty.

They have seen that Ireland got the chance to vote – twice, thanks to Brussels' refusal to take No for an answer – and they want a referendum of their own.

Significantly, four out of ten of those polled would

tear up ALL our treaties with Europe and quit the union immediately.

That proportion would almost certainly grow if Tony Blair were picked, unelected, as the first EU President over the heads of the British people.

It is the prospect of an IN-or-OUT vote that terrifies the Tories who are apparently heading for power next Spring.

Party leader David Cameron knows the Irish YES vote leaves Britain a lonely and isolated voice against the universally detested Constitution.

He is hoping against hope that the Czechs can withhold their final endorsement until he rides to their rescue.

But he knows Czech President Václav Klaus is under intense pressure to capitulate, despite Mr Cameron's pledge to hold a referendum if he hangs on.

Once the treaty is in place, any British vote will be tantamount to a referendum on our continued membership.

And there is every prospect of a resounding vote for withdrawal.

To be fair, that would be a nightmare for a newly-elected government, opening an unwelcome second front as it struggles to save the UK economy from meltdown.

But this is no zero sum game. It would also terrify those who rule the EU as an unaccountable, unrepresentative and undemocratic elite.

The political state of Europe has much more to lose from a British referendum.

The United Kingdom might be seen by the federalists as carping irritants.

But realists know our departure – or even a majority-backed threat to depart – would rock the Union to its foundations and threaten its future.

Sixty-one million British voters, once they have spoken, could not be ignored.

Our neighbours may love us or loathe us but, along with Germany and France, we are one of the Big Three – without whom the EU jigsaw is incomplete.

We may be the awkward squad, but many states – including even France and Germany – are frequently grateful for our lateral way of seeing things.

More to the point, our taxpayers contribute a large chunk of the cash the EU needs to run its increasingly chaotic, corrupt and costly operations. After all, we pay in much more than we take out.

And, for all their threats, there is nothing serious they could do to stop us leaving. Yes, we would have to unpick countless directives, statutory instruments and regulations. But there is no treaty that cannot be revoked.

Our trade – with UK imports of €229 billion far outstripping €177bn of exports – is far too valuable for Europe to jeopardise through petty retaliation. Not to mention the risk of breaching World Trade Organisation rules.

Could we manage on our own?

Lee Rotherham argues persuasively that we could do better than that.

In his vision of Britain "Ten Years On", he sees a

nation liberated from the dead hand of EU bureaucracy.

A nation where we can fish our own, richly-resuscitated coastal waters.

Where our farmers are set free to feed the people instead of being driven to the brink of bankruptcy by crazy diktats from Brussels.

A country where we can determine our own civil and criminal laws and reach our own conclusions on human rights and health and safety without having them dictated to us.

A country that could decide its own immigration policy and defend itself militarily without asking permission from 26 bickering heads of government.

Most important of all, as Tony Benn keeps saying, we will know who is in charge – and if we don't like the way they do the job, we can kick 'em out.

Properly governed and freed from faceless Euro-cratic control, Britain should thrive and prosper as a free nation state once more.

Imagine how that would go down with 450 million European citizens locked into a totalitarian museum-state, deprived of a say in their own affairs and watching a newly liberated ex-partner showing how it can be done.

# Part One: 2020 – Views from a Free Country

Time is an illusion, and the historian a great sorcerer. This is the story of the past, as we live through it from today.

It was the event of the generation. Here in 2020, many of us who are old enough can think back 30 years to reflect upon the seismic shift of our youth; the shudder that heralded the end of the Cold War, the death throes of Soviet communism, and the breaking of the dual Europe – the continent of the armed camps, the steel legions and the iron walls.

But that had been long years ago, filled with lost promise.

2010 had been the year of the aftershock – tectonic in British history, and vital and invigorating beyond these storm-tussled shores. The United Kingdom found itself, as much by accident as by design, freed of the cloying molasses of Brussels.

And with its regained freedom, Britain had prospered.

This is a narrative of that decade of success, and the tragedy of the lost years that preceded it: the Babylonian Captivity of the British economy.

# Part One: 2020 – Views from a free Country

# The Business Owner

Sheila Jones runs a successful small business, *Gentle Breezes*, in Birmingham. Over the past twelve months, it has expanded and taken on two new members of staff. Unlike a few years ago, the paperwork that went with this has not proved such a major irritant.

There is a very good reason for this. The amount of red tape choking business in Britain has gone down. The process of review began within weeks of breaking with the old EU structures. It was no easy task; there were thousands upon thousands of statutory instruments, putting into law 105,000 pages of European regulations. These needed to be sifted to determine which ones were commonsensical, which ones were superfluous, and which went way beyond the original intent and were simply damaging. There were a lot that fell into the last category. The review quickly revealed just how many bad laws went far beyond the original EU intent, because the civil service had added to the text for reasons of its own.

Tens of thousands of pages of regulations were correspondingly either simplified or cut. Businesses were amongst the major winners. Mrs Jones found that she had two hours less paperwork to fill out every week. The health and safety paperwork was much clearer, and based on common sense.

One example was the legislation governing waste disposal. The concept was a popular one, but the old rules governing it seemed at times to have been drafted on another planet. A small firm was expected to cough up £850 in a given year to be compliant with just one directive, with a wall of paperwork that seemed to push waste to travel further while encouraging local fly tipping. These compliance costs were passed on to the consumer, without even counting the extra £15 per tonne to dispose of the waste.

In some cases, lightening the legislation while keeping the intent rubbed away much of the gold plating; in others, the bureaucracy was so heavy for so little benefit it was just dumped. Nationally, the clear out over several years was judged to have saved two per cent of the country's GDP. That totted up to a staggering £19 billion. In Mrs Jones' case two per cent extra income meant expanding the company this year.

Thanks to the trade agreement reached with the EU, her company continues to deal with the same partners on the continent as she had prior to 2010. The punishing tariffs some had feared as the price for UK independence never materialised, because it was never in the interests of business partners to cut off their own nose to spite their face. So Gabi from Frankfurt still calls once a week, while Aleix and Llora in Barcelona have increased their orders on last year's thanks to the striking new floral design that's proven quite a hit.

But then, as with most companies, eight tenths of her business was with shops in Penrith, Southend and other parts of the UK, and another tenth with the States and Australia and countries elsewhere outside the EU. The red tape forced on her from Brussels a decade back was affecting all of her business while only intended to make life easier for one tenth of it, so the burden was mismatched.

A sign of the times this week was the phone call from Shanghai. The city's economic growth this year is practically double that of the national Chinese average, and even that was at 6.9 per cent. There are potentially thousands of new consumers interested in buying her products in that city alone, who this year now have the jobs and the money. Truly, the future is bigger than just the EU, it is global.

# The Workforce

Ashley Grayson is one of those whose been taken on at *Gentle Breezes*. He's a school leaver who decided that university wasn't for him. His girlfriend Nikki is a student at college who already has an eye on a year abroad. Again, the programmes that allowed British and foreign students to spend time overseas didn't come crashing to a halt in 2010, which was hardly surprising considering that so many exchange programmes took place with countries not in the EU in the first place. So Nikki has her eye on a year at Nantes to improve her French.

Ashley is happy with his job and his prospects. When he wants to do overtime to cover the bills, he can. The EU regulations that prevent his counterpart on the continent from working more than 48 hours a week (soon to be dropped to 44) don't apply to the UK, so Ashley is free to choose to put in for overtime to suit his own needs, which he expects will next be around December. That said, since it's a small business and sometimes orders come in thick and fast, he doesn't mind the occasional weekend blitz in order to help the boss out, not least if it pays for going with the girlfriend to Miami rather than Ibiza this year. If he lived and worked in Strasbourg, on the other hand, he and his boss would have been breaking the law. The company (and his bank manager) would have had to lump it.

Ashley knows that a job these days is no longer for life. The UK has employment regulations very different from those in the EU. There, the emphasis is on keeping jobs rather than building new ones. What that means, however, is that in downturns businesses in trouble – and especially small businesses – are far less able to adapt to change. They aren't able to lay off people for a few months in order to cut overheads and weather the storm. EU politicians have yet to learn the lessons of the last recession, where shocking numbers of new small business folded because they couldn't adapt to the economic climate. Unable to bend, they snapped.

That wasn't just bad news for the people who owned and ran the companies, it was catastrophic news for the employees. For the sake of preserving the privileges of millions of workers, hundreds of thousands had to lose their jobs.

In Britain, unemployment levels had gone up much more quickly, but then recovered with far greater speed. Moreover, here businesses found themselves far more competitive. This was doubly true with respect to those countries where governments had decided to massively subsidise the key state industries, rather than force them to finally get round to the structural changes that had been made in other countries in the 1980s. In other words, taxpayers there were paying higher taxes to support big industries, which were exporting products overseas, providing cheap raw materials for workers in other countries to manufacture at a competitive profit. The whole system was messy on the eye and heavy on the wallet – but not in Britain.

By 2020, the EU law grinder has been churning overtime in this area. Brussels has implemented a wide package of provisions eked out of the Social Charter. On the continent, there has been a massive leap in court cases of employees seeking wage rises for menial or unpleasant work, thanks to laws supposedly relating to fair pay. Parents, including men, have won increasingly absurd cases under legislation relating to family rights, allowing them to knock off work early, or for one over-protective mother to check up on her child at school. Attempts to reform social security pay were halted by a European Court of Justice ruling that docking money from a work-shy father would have interfered with his 'rights'. New regulations govern time spent in stressful locations, such as overly-rigid requirements for breaks when working while seated, also leading to chaos on building sites when people clocked in differently. At least that provision was reversed quickly after it came in 2017, but the restoration of sympathetic striking, and the legal requirement for vocational training in a subject of the jobseeker's choice (including one notorious case as a Buddhist nun), both remain on the books.

MEPs are the worst offenders, taking every advantage of their increasing power to push new laws. In the pipeline at the European Parliament are complex proposals grading types of work in order to increase the pay of women cleaners, matching them to male employees in the same office, in part based on length of employment. So too are rules requiring companies to employ a percentile of staff who are under 21, over 60, and the disabled. None of these laws applies in the UK.

Health and safety, needless to say, has been a celebrated nightmare. Still, if nothing else, it has spawned a well-paid, outspoken and highly certified growth industry, employing hundreds of thousands of people across the EU. Some of the brightest minds in Europe are global leaders in creating warning designs intelligible across borders, alerting people not to spill hot water.

## Lawed To Death

Laws covering working conditions have led to countless directives. The drafts didn't need too much research. Some of the paperwork first came from the regulations already governing Brussels' own bureaucrats back in 2004. The Commission's *Manual of Standard Building Standards* has long spelled out in minute detail the quality controls that the Commission had to employ in decking out its own buildings, containing such requirements as the following – "Modular Configuration Of Office Space: Many years of experience in the use of office space have led us to conclude that the ideal architectural module of office space is 1.20 metres, but could be between 1.20 and 1.40 metres in width".

In such circumstances, no detail is insignificant; "The architectural design of buildings should take account of the following requirements:

- furniture delivery
- the arrangement of furniture in the different areas of the building, and
- the need for floor and wall coverings that are resistant to shocks caused by the use and transport of furniture."

Or can go to the other extreme. Try this data on ceilings; "The following minimum heights are considered ideal: technical facilities in attic areas: h = 3.0 m; office areas: h = 2.6 m; ground floor: h = 3.5 m; basement floors: h = 2.2 m."

Now we can start to see an inkling of what the system is fundamentally about: the regulation of the infinitesimal. Under "Sound insulation," a Health & Safety warden might read, for instance, "Four tests are to be carried out in-situ by an approved body to measure the airborne insulation of partitions between offices, and between offices and corridors." It continues with noise pollution that, "the composition of walls, ceilings and other reflective surfaces must be such that the time difference between the arrival of incident sound and reflected sound is less than 0.02 seconds."

No item under the process escapes regulation: "Each door should comprise a frame (made of wood, metal or prefabricated sections) and a door leaf (consisting of a solid wooden core with extra-hard facing panels, wooden edges and edge-strips, finished with decorative paint or panels, or enameled sheet-steel facing)." It continues, "The decorative facing should consist of laminated plates, natural wood panels (varnished or stained European maple), sheet steel or thermolacquered sheet aluminium around glazed sections. The minimum breadth should be 93cm and the minimum height 201.5cm."

Of course, it doesn't stop there: there are the handles. "These should be U-shaped with a diameter of 20mm, a length of approximately 135mm and a projection of 70mm. They should be attached by means of pressure screws and mounted on two circular rosettes. Locks fitted with devices indicating 'vacant/occupied' should be of the same diameter and should be equipped with a knob on the inside for operating the red and white disc indicator visible on the outside of the door; provision must be made for unlocking these doors from the outside with an emergency key or coin [. . ./. . .] Door handles should be made of coloured nylon material and reinforced along their full length. The nylon should have a smooth, non-porous surface resistant to oil, detergent, acid and disinfectant and should be non-flammable and noncombustible. A selection of colours should be available so that door fittings can be harmonised with the colours of other fittings and the doors themselves."

There are no privy secrets either. "The toilets are to be made of white porcelain. The flush mechanism is to be as quiet as possible and have a maximum capacity of 9 litres, with a manual button (marked with text or a pictogram) to stop the flush. Flush flow: 6 l, adjustable. [. . ./. . .] The urinals must be installed at a height suitable for persons of average size."

Nothing so easily encapsulates the essence of Brussels than these old rules governing the Commission's own offices – all 398 pages of them.

But outside of the downpour of EU regulations, in self-governing Britain, Sheila Jones and Ashley Grayson can simply get on with their jobs – keeping *Gentle Breezes* in business, trading across Britain and the world.

# The Representative

Part of the reason for Britain's success compared with EU competitors boils down to a single word: *accountability*. Another word for it is *democracy*.

The true meaning and value of these abstracts can often be hard to appreciate. But the local MP for Sheila and Ashley understands it perfectly.

Graham Peal was first elected for the constituency back in 2010. He is a former teacher – a deputy head, in fact. Not surprisingly, he got into politics first and foremost because of education issues, but also over the dire state of the economy.

Looking back, Mr Peal admits that his views have changed somewhat. "I remember before I got involved in politics, watching the television news back in the early 1990s. When the Maastricht debate was tearing politicians apart, I recall just turning to my wife and saying, 'Look at that bunch of nutters. They just haven't got a clue about the real world.' It seemed to me at the time that it was like kids in the playground scrapping over trading cards or something."

Peal's view shifted when he got elected, thanks to some first hand experience of what the EU in practical terms meant. "I'd scarcely been in for a month I guess. First there was the euphoria of getting in, you know the adrenaline of this great change in your life, and then all the paperwork and chaos about getting the office up and running. But then the constituency case work started to kick in. That's when reality struck.

"I got this letter from a constituent who was complaining that the local council was collecting the dustbins every fortnight. He'd contacted them, who said that it wasn't their fault, but they were following new rules. So he wanted to know if as an MP I could change them if the council couldn't. Looking into the problem, I found that the root of the issue lay in a European Directive on landfill dating back to 1999, designed to massively cut it, but that councils were not able to find the resources to fund disposing of the waste in other, greener but more costly, ways.

"Next was a phone call from this bloke who was concerned about something he'd read in his business trade magazine, about changes to employment rules on short term workers. My researcher soon found out that at source there was an EU Agency Workers Directive, so there was nothing I, as this guy's MP, could do to affect that one.

"Next day, the one straight after the other, I had a lady complaining how she had been in a queue for a hip operation and it was in the local press how someone had leapfrogged her and gone straight over to France and booked themselves in over there, expecting the NHS to pay thanks to a ruling by the European Court of Justice; and then I had a fireman worried about the threat of including his stand-by time with the time he worked when calculating the amount of hours he was allowed to be on duty. Well, that last one was yet again under threat despite us supposedly having an opt-out from the Working Time Directive, and that affected doctors too, and in the patch of one of my colleagues I'm told the local lifeboat station, not counting the armed forces.

"It was a wake up call. In the space of a week I discovered just how much Brussels really ran. Sure,

13

MPs would sign things off on the dotted line as a formality thing, but the real decision making was done by civil servants in committee rooms miles away from elected politicians. Even Ministers were generally out of the loop until the negotiations were well under way, by which time it was pretty difficult to do anything radical about them. Especially in all those areas where we had given up the veto."

Mr Peal was not very impressed with the old attitude of some of his colleagues who had lived through this experience. "One of my colleagues used to say that only nine per cent of Britain's laws were made in Brussels. Well, that's fine if you only count the British laws that were passed in order to make EU laws formal. But that's a tiny portion of the lot, so that's a very cheeky deception. The Belgian Government put it at 40 per cent as coming from drafts in Brussels. Looking at the inspirations for laws increased the figure. The German President said that, adding all the direct and indirect root sources of lawmaking together, 84 per cent of laws originated from EU institutions.

"The scale was massive. I made a list out of it. If you traded something, made something, sold something, ran something, policed something, protected something, transported something, communicated something, floated something, fished something, grew something, burnt something, buried something, stored something, repaired something, bought something, spent something, exchanged something, taught something, learned something, appreciated something, walked something, powered something, healed something, published something, sponsored something, researched something, reported something, supported something . . . well, you get the picture. The European Commission was everywhere, EU laws were everywhere, and the scope was getting bigger with every new treaty. MPs, Parliament, we came way down the food chain."

Mr Peal backs up his point with some statistics. In 2009, there were 30,000 legal acts on the EU's books. There were also 10,000 verdicts reached by the European Court of Justice at Luxembourg, interpreting how they were applied, and 40,000 sets of agreed international standards. That made 89,962 in total. Even allowing for only a proportion of these to be ones that would later be repealed, the scale of the problem was clear. Twenty or thirty items were going past ministers every month as "A Points" just on the nod. No wonder that the parliamentary scrutiny committee that used to rubber stamp the regulations used to meet in secret: the truth was too embarrassing for the public to behold.

But compare the situation now in 2020, with Britain free.

When a law is drafted, it is worked on by British civil servants from the outset. It is tailored for British needs, rather than attempting to suit an economy running from Lapland to Benidorm.

The process is mandated and managed by British ministers, who are responsible for it. Ministers go before Parliament and are held accountable for bad laws, and can no longer fob off complaints that this was someone else's law and, while they didn't like it was voted through and what could they do? Now that excuse was gone: bad laws cost them their job.

Constituents knew it. The added transparency has helped to clear up politics. In 2017, a former minister was even deselected by his own party association over one scandalously mismanaged Bill that a businessman had effectively tried to bribe into law. Under the old European system on the contrary, you had European Commissioners in charge who had actually been indicted for fraud.

Ten years ago, Brussels was turning into Washington DC; a Las Vegas for lobbyists and the big game hunters of transcontinental lawmaking, while the little man waited outside. Westminster on the other hand was turning into Cardiff.

Today, when Mr Peal's constituents ring up to complain about waste management, short term contract work, the way the NHS works, and working hours, they expect him to get onto the case and do something about it. Because he can.

# The Fisherman

Jim Thomson is rightly proud of his new thirty footer. Riding high in the dockside at Peterhead, the *Annie* is the newest addition to the Scottish fishing fleet. Along with two other recently built vessels in the harbour, it symbolises the painfully slow recovery facing the industry today in 2020, after a period of 40 years of decline.

Back in 1970, there had been 21,443 fishermen in the UK, with around one in seven of the workforce working part time. By the time Britain left the EU, there were just over 12,000.

Four in ten jobs at sea had been lost. But the damage was far more widespread, because there were ten jobs sustained on land maintaining the boats and processing what they caught. All told, the Common Fisheries Policy (CFP) had cost British coastal communities 115,000 jobs.

They went in part because the fish went, and in part because new fishermen moved in from other EU countries. The bitter truth was that this was a resource that under international law, run outside of the EEC, would have been preserved for the local workforce. Norwegian politicians saw the writing on the wall long ago; the fisheries minister in 1972 resigned rather than support his government in wrecking the fishing industry, and his analysis was key in persuading his countrymen that EEC membership was a bad deal.

But British politicians concealed this harsh pill. So while in 1973, 1,110,096 tonnes of fish were being landed from British vessels, by 2006 that had dropped to 615,780 tonnes.

In the last ten years of membership alone, the number of UK fishing vessels fell by 20 per cent. Capacity fell by over a fifth in tonnage, while engine power dropped by a sixth. That was not all. New boats were not being built. By 2008, more vessels dated from before Britain even joined the EEC than had been built over the last decade. Well over half were twenty or thirty years old.

But this contrasted with the fleets of their competitors, especially the Spanish. During the heyday of grants handed out to upgrade fishing boats and ports, awash with hundreds of millions, for every Pound the British got to make their fishermen competitive, the Portuguese got an extra 43p, the French 54p, and the Spanish . . . £6.72. In Spain's case, these grants went towards replacing about 1,400 obsolete vessels, and the modernization of about 1,800 existing ones. They had to fish somewhere, and Britain's traditional fishing grounds would soon legally be theirs as well.

Given the UK's share of the budget and the exchange rate, this equated to around £150million of UK taxpayers' money alone having gone to support foreign fishermen under this one scheme. The grants continued in different forms, meaning that even after they were supposed to have concluded, British taxpayers continued to subsidise other countries' fishing industries to the tune of £64 million a year.

Nor were the recipients of grants in Britain necessarily British fishermen. Under one in fifty British fishing boats was foreign owned, but because these were the biggest boats, they made up about a sixth of the tonnage. Attempts to get round foreign flagging and pay UK-designated grants only to UK-owned vessels had famously fallen apart in the 1990 *Factortame* court case, resulting in hefty compensation settlements. The whole scheme was a fiasco, as British taxpayers weren't even subsidising British vessel owners in their own national quota allocations, let alone the subsidy rates forked out openly to owners in Brest or Bilbao.

Bluntly put, it meant that over the course of the last century, the UK fishing fleet, and its associated industries, has been crippled on three occasions; by the Kaiser, by Hitler, and by the Common Fisheries Policy. By 2009, landings of fish were barely above the levels of 1915, when the North Sea was a war zone.

The bill for this state of affairs was no less scandalous. Unemployment in the fleet and in support industries had added £138 million to the social security budget of the nation. The decline in fishing communities had massive social implications, devaluing them by £27 million as judged by insurance valuations. The recreational fishing industry faced the prospect of new legislation that even on a low estimate looked like £11 million in lost revenue thanks to the prospect of new levels of bureaucracy. £65 million went in different forms of support to foreign industries. £12 million to the European Commission to buy licences, mostly for the Spanish to fish out third world waters. The costs went on and on and on.

The fishermen were not the only ones paying the price. Many of these costs carried across to the till, not least because of the scarcity of the produce. The average household ended up paying £186 each year, or £3.58 a week, extra as a result. That of course was on top of the prices added to their checkout costs through the quite separate Common Agricultural Policy fiasco.

At the same time, the ecological impact of the CFP was utterly scandalous. Jim Thomson's counterparts in Grimsby, Hull and Boston recall with horror the old rules that used to bind them at sea, including one famous regulation that made them rub each individual fish's belly to tell young herring and sprats apart – quite a job when you had a full hold.

The Government's own estimates from 2007 recalled that for that <u>one</u> year alone, in <u>just</u> the North Sea area, and just looking at <u>three</u> types of fish, 23,600 tonnes of cod, 31,048 tonnes of haddock, and 6,000 tonnes of whiting were caught and then simply thrown back dead over the side of the boat, to drop to the sea floor and pollute the bed. It was a humiliation even Soviet Commissars could never have dreamed up.

It meant that over three times the cod limit authorised by Brussels for British fishermen was dumped, six sevenths the British total for haddock, and two thirds of the UK whiting permitted catch.

That 60,000 tonnes of dumped fish was enough to fill a 200 metre long supramax bulk carrier ship, or keep Billingsgate fish market stocked for two and a half years.

Perhaps it was easier to visualise it in weight terms another way. The United Nations Food and Agriculture Organisation put its total estimates of North Sea discards at up to 880,000 tonnes. That in weight terms was the equivalent of harpooning 200 sperm whales every month, and then just leaving them to float dead in the sea.

It was hardly surprising that on Britain's leaving the CFP, DEFRA (the responsible government ministry) immediately halted all dumping at sea and required all fish to be landed. That in itself did not immediately rescue the industry; the scandal had been going on for too long. There had been the industrial dredging of sand eels, a key component of the marine food chain, for use as Danish pig food. With collapses in key stocks, species had shifted, in some places with jellyfish moving in as the dominant local species with disastrous consequences for the fishing industry. Even sea bird populations had been affected, with some replaced by aggressive species that flourished on discards. Some species of fish had meanwhile only managed to survive by adapting their very biology, physically maturing and spawning years earlier, such was the scale of the cataclysm.

DEFRA's policy change had an immediate economical effect, as £130 million of fish that would otherwise have been dumped at sea now was landed. This was the initial one-off bonanza. A new system then came into play involving the 'carry over' of quota, negotiated at local community level. Where boats caught more than they were supposed to over the course of the season – typically accidentally as a result of fishing for other species – the catch would still be landed, weighed in order to add to the scientific understanding of the stocks, sold, and then reduced from the allowed catch limit for the following year.

With no longer a third of fish being caught and

dumped, the stock slowly began to replenish. It has been a long process, and will take many long years yet to approach anything like the levels prior to joining the EEC, but the statistics are clear. Allowing the previously dumped fish to grow to maturity by this form of management doubles the stock size by the time they reach the age to spawn. So Britain's territorial waters, now reclaimed, have scraped past a Grand Banks-style fisheries collapse, but only just.

Other species are also better off. In December 2004, DEFRA unilaterally banned British vessels from pelagic pair trawling for bass. This form of fishing unfortunately had the side effect of catching cetaceans. However, under CFP rules, it couldn't ban foreign vessels in most of what are now British waters. DEFRA's 2010 blanket ban in favour of gillnetting and handlining is estimated today to save some 592 porpoises and 114 dolphins from drowning in nets every year.

## Hard Tack

It was not particularly savvy of the Spanish to have picked this particular issue as the *casus belli* for the one major dispute over Britain's post-EU treaty terms. Ministers in Madrid had anticipated one of several trigger points, and were prepared to fight a major battle to protect the rights accrued by their fishermen over the preceding 20 years. Intending to wage a sort of Cod War mark two, Madrid found it difficult instead to overcome the image of being Flipper-bashing pirates. Nevertheless, on a local level there was innate sympathy for some of the skippers who had become familiar faces in the pubs of Newquay, Fleetwood and the rest, whom local British fishermen knew and in whom they saw an affinity.

True, there were some hot headed moments, occasioned by the suspicion that the *MV Burgos* was 'klondyking' and ferrying caught fish directly back from the fishing vessel to a Spanish port. There was the run in with the French over the Guernsey grounds, leading to a retaliatory incident at Lerwick where the boat owner was locked in with the herring overnight. Then Dublin joined in over Spanish incursions into the Irish Box. Jolly Rogers flew in support from the masts of vessels in the harbours of Newfoundland and Nova Scotia.

The presence of Russian boats new to the waters demonstrated that the situation needed to be quickly resolved. At a round table summit in Edinburgh, the 200 mile limit (or median line where waters overlapped) was confirmed as lying under British sovereignty, as was already clear under international law. Owners that had an historic pre-1973 access were allowed to continue as before (this affected a handful of French, Belgians, Dutch and Scandinavian owners). Skippers who had arrived since then, however, would only be allowed continued access for their lifetimes, though they would have equal rights in local community meetings that discussed how the fishing ground was run.

Jim Thomson's new boat is a sign of the confidence that is now re-emerging in 2020. Leaving the CFP meant that the industry was freed from much of the £22 million of red tape burdens. Lower food prices have led to the public paying £269 million less every year in taxes through food bills factored into social security payouts. Millions of pounds are still being recouped every year by skippers selling fish they would otherwise have been dumping dead back into the sea.

It is a long way from the £2.1 billion British fishermen had lost by home waters rights being surrendered, and even further from correcting the £2.8 billion that was the total economic cost of the CFP while it was running. However, says Jim, come the next generation, when *Annie* is old and rusting and about to be cut up, you'll see. The stocks will be back, the harbours will be filled, the foreign boats mostly gone, and the ports will be alive once more.

# The British Farmer

Ten years on, and the world of agriculture has changed. Leaving the old European Union meant Britain dropping the Common Agricultural Policy. What happened initially was that the UK ended funding for the central CAP budget and set up its own UK-CAP in parallel.

At the outset, DEFRA – also the UK's ministry for agriculture – simply match-funded existing grants paid out in the UK while future policy was debated. Yet this simple action saved British taxpayers one billion pounds a year, through no longer having UK taxes subsidising foreign farmers.

Meanwhile, facing a four year reduction in the CAP budget and an unwillingness to fund French farmers, the remaining EU countries shifted to a part-state funded system to plug the gap. Over the long term, this proved a massive spark to reform. As national taxpayers in France, Spain, Italy and Germany felt for the first time in decades that they themselves were paying to subsidise food, and more expensive food at that, they began to take a direct interest in what was going on. Members of the public felt that as it was their money, it should be spent well. MPs also started to realise that their constituents were not all working on farms. Movements for reform now began to spring up across the continent, popular campaigns that would in time lead to real change. Protectionism in world agriculture now had a popular *best before* label and a shelf life.

Back in Britain, DEFRA meanwhile was facing a policy revolution. British farmers and consumer groups were at loggerheads. The National Farmers Union was close to civil war, as smallholders, lease-holders, hill farmers and grain barons clashed.

Given the turmoil, it was inevitable a compromise was reached, at least over the transitional period. But look at where we are today in 2020.

Eric Parker is planning on retiring from farming next year. A few years ago he was saying that the business was a mug's game. Yet now he is happy that his son, Bill, is stepping up to the mark. The reforms that Britain made as long ago as the late 1970s have set the UK a good 30 years ahead of its continental competitors, who are anticipating major farm mergers and takeovers.

One reform that British farming ministers were able to swiftly implement outside of the CAP was to retarget where agricultural aid ended up. In the past, too many recipients were not the intended beneficiaries. Rather than borderline farming communities who were still struggling in the aftermath of the latest cull of all their breeding stock, historically support had favoured the grain barons. Back in the 1980s, four fifths of the benefits had ended up directed towards one fifth of the farmers, simply because of their volume of output, and despite the fact that efficiency of scale removed the need for most of this support.

Subsequent CAP reforms had failed to remove much of the sting. On far too many occasions large sums had also ended up as surprise subsidies for the eclectic. Between 2002 and 2007, CAP recipients included £223,000 for a defence laboratory; £112,000 for the London Borough of Tower Hamlets; £88,000 for a hotel chain; £42,000 for a coal mine; £28,000 for a gypsum mining company; £27,000 for British Telecom; £16,000 for a water company; £14,000 for a horse trainer; £5,000 for Eton College; not to mention thousands of pounds for caravan sites, museums, cathedrals, airfields, sports clubs and so on. From now on, you didn't get farming aid if you played tennis on it or landed a plane on it. You got it if, like Eric Parker, you grew on it, and the market was rough.

Another swift change was less to do with policy, and everything to do with clarity. No longer dependent upon the Commission and the Council of Ministers to agree to decisions, the speed of decision-making accelerated considerably. This proved critical in the brief suspected outbreak of contagious bovine pleuropneumonia in 2014, where a highly localised cull accompanied by swift vaccination and registration of nearby livestock avoided another Foot and Mouth fiasco. The chain of authorisation had been clear from the outset. Even the chary NFU acknowledged that the 72 hours saved on the old mechanism had proved critical.

Other changes have been more gradual. Fifty years ago, the UK was mostly self-sufficient in milk. Under the CAP, the system had become so corrupted that many British farmers had turned to dealing in quotas rather than sell milk at depressed UK gate prices. Outside of the old EU treaties, British ministers had been able to instigate reforms to rescue the dairy industry. Quotas suppressing British production in favour of guaranteed French imports had ended. Livestock breeding was re-emerging as a profitable industry thanks to increased demand in the markets of East

Asia, particularly China which is starting to buy into British dairy produce, just as world food prices increase again. Thanks to a major public push by the *Ethical British Produce* campaign in 2014, headed up by the ubiquitously marvellous Joanna Lumley, super-markets were shamed into negotiating an extra 4p in the pint deal with farmers, also guaranteeing a profit margin with suppliers in the future, in return for dairy farmers supporting basic *Compassion in World Farming* principles.

EU food mountains developed in an unexpected way. In 2008, the Commission had begun to rebuild them, albeit compared with past amounts as mere foothills rather than Alpine fastnesses. 30,000 tonnes of butter and 109,000 tonnes of skimmed powder milk joined 2.3 million hectolitres of inferior wine, or enough to fill around 92 Olympic sized swimming pools.

Leaving the CAP ended intervention, but it did not completely end food storage. A British government review in 2013 reached the conclusion that supply-orientated food provision carried major social risks. To recall the old maxim, society was only three meals away from a revolution. Since the amount of food in the supply chain at any one time ran to an emergency reserve of half a loaf per person, it was decided a special contingency reserve ought to be constituted. This would be made up of long-term imperishable foodstuffs, which would be released in case of a major transport strike, interruption of shipping, or difficulties arising due to war. Farmers producing cannable produce did well out of the arrangement, though the feedback from those who received stocks after the

Naples earthquake proved that it was, like wartime Spam, an acquired taste.

Nevertheless, that was a strategy of choice. The policy of spending millions effectively to speculate on food stocks, leading to them being offloaded on third countries as subsidies, did end. Other costs also diminished. With a simpler system, administration costs for the grants were less onerous. The old CAP had sapped £72 million just in wage costs for the main civil servants running it. Their furniture allowance alone every year ran to £5.4 million.

Nor did the UK have to continue subsidising southern European tobacco farmers hundreds of millions of pounds to grow sub-standard crop for dumping on third world markets, since the Cairngorms proved unsurprisingly short in plantations.

Britain's share of other CAP insanities also fell away. Part of £5.6 million spent on promoting produce, in an industry where every human being has no choice but to be a consumer. Another £5.6 million spent on PR for the CAP, or "enhancing public awareness" as it was euphemistically known. £108 million provided in direct aid to producer organisations, seemingly selected on their ability to lobby. Perhaps after all it was no coincidence that under the old system, £12 million had been set aside for cases where the European Commission might be sued and fined for mismanagement.

The more straightforward system in the UK also encouraged ministers to cut back on the regulations. Eric Parker stopped getting endless packages of paperwork through the post five years ago. Farmers across Britain are able to get on with their jobs without filling out endless forms to prove that they had complied with health and safety minutiae, and rely instead on basic rules and common sense. Burdensome laws, such as those that required fallen livestock to be transported away in a manner not far short of befitting a lost relative, were repealed. The net result was that ten years of over-intrusive red tape was removed, and farm businesses across the land were collectively £264 million better off.

# The Third World Farmer

But Mr Parker is not the only person better off. Twenty miles out of Orapa, in Botswana, Tebogo Melesi is also a farmer. His cattle continue to be subject to tariffs under the EU market, excepting only some several hundred tonnes of beef across the whole country that are allowed preferential EU treatment each year. He remembers the disappointment of hearing on the radio about how the failure of the talks at Doha, halfway around the planet, meant that nobody wanted to buy his produce in Europe while on the streets of the capital Gaborone subsidised (and sometimes simply dumped) European beef was competing with his own.

Although he doesn't know why, this year he was able to sell one more heifer than usual. The gradual freeing up of the European, and particularly British, markets to competition will in time mean that European aid donors will be able to retarget £400 million of aid lately spent simply on compensating subsistence farmers. Tebogo's little daughter, Kefilwe, will go to a new school next summer.

Across the border, the farms of Zimbabwe are starting to get back into action. With the passing of Mugabe and the so-called "Suitcase Revolution", President Tsvangirai prioritised the rescue of the collapsed farm sector, combining restitution, long-term compensation, and tenant review. The British Government was able, within 36 hours of the President taking office, to underwrite the investment process by guaranteeing tariff-free exports to Britain for the first seven years, helping to settle the markets and shake off the prospect of a ZANU coup.

It took the European Union Agriculture Council four weeks to even discuss it.

# The Consumer

In the last year of its operation, the Common Agricultural Policy cost Britain £10.3 billion a year. It accounted for around five per cent of the price of food.

Around half, £4.7 billion, came from the cost of the British taxpayer subsidising farmers (over a fifth of this, one billion pounds, subsidising farmers directly on behalf of another country's taxpayers).

An estimated £317 million was also spent on the increased costs of welfare benefits paid out, since the state had to pay people on welfare extra to compensate for the higher price of food that it itself had caused.

Protectionism also pushed up the price of food in the UK by an estimated £5.3 billion, since tariffs were added to cheap imports to make them no longer competitive on the shelves.

Since joining the EEC, the price of cheddar cheese had gone up fourteen fold; imported lamb thirteen fold; a loaf of white bread tenfold; imported butter ninefold; and rump steak by a factor of seven.

For a family like the Aroras in Ealing who have two children, that meant paying £398 pounds every year. Broken down even further, that was the equivalent of adding around £7.65 per week to their family food bill.

With the country in a recession, ten years ago the Aroras would have found their family budget very tight. With world food prices falling from their exceptional commodity high, the protectionist cost of the CAP was once again increasingly exposed. Saving £400 a year, over one per cent of the household's post-tax income, would have been a real relief.

The decision to partially open up British markets to imports, while cushioning the blow for farmers, fell short of the flashbang reforms pioneered by the New Zealand government, and indeed fell disappointingly short of the measures called for by the Cairns Group of low tariff agricultural exporters, but it did prove a significant first step. The Aroras weren't paying Auckland prices, to be sure. That would have led to sausages being a third cheaper, and sirloin in the trolley for less than the old price of rump. But even a partial reform, half achieved, saved £200. It was the equivalent of a couple of weeks' shopping for the family that paid for itself. That paid for the children's school uniforms and new shoes last year. This year, it'll half cover the water rates. Next year, perhaps it'll go into the car insurance.

£400, thinks Mrs Arora, would go further.

# The Law Enforcer

The Sorensen Gang hit the headlines in 2014. This trio of desperados, wanted in three EU countries for armed robberies and wounding, made a break for it across the Channel.

They carried fake Euro-IDs, which at the time were recognised as passport equivalents (a failing since repealed now everyone knows that the continental ID card system is just as forgeable as the €500 note). What they forgot was that, even though the UK is outside of the Schengen and Europol systems, it has always cooperated closely with the institutions in sharing intelligence. Tipped off by their counterparts, ENSIS identified the gang's location; Special Branch and CO19 moved in for the arrest; a judge reviewed the case for removal; the three were extradited.

Leaving the old EU treaty didn't mean Britain ending cooperation with EU countries; it meant keeping it to cooperation that's under British management on British turf. In a global economy, with globalised criminal networks operating across borders, and hiding their stash in investments and bank accounts around the world, global cooperation is key. In that sense, in justice matters as in many others, it is the EU that is small.

Many of the same lessons could be drawn from the Lazami network, controlling a chunk of the Balkans smuggling circuit, which was lifted in 2016 thanks to cooperation between a number of agencies including two based in London. Again, there were the headlines in 2017 relating to the breaking of an international child kidnapping and abuse ring in La Paz. In each of these cases, as in a thousand more, success came not from having a unified European entity. Indeed, in many cases, success only came from involving non-European actors. But it was about commonality of approach, and sensible cooperation.

The major difference today is one of public confidence.

Look back to when Britain was in the EU. If a judge in another country had signed a European Arrest Warrant, so long as the form was filled out correctly, the British police would have been required to collect the individual and deliver him overseas. Shockingly, it was only in early 2009, after several years in operation, that a particular box was added to the form, one that related to people who had been convicted in absentia. This required the judge to state if the person had originally been given fair warning that he had been on trial!

Outside of the EU, Britain's opt-out from the Justice and Home Affairs provisions, shaky under the more authoritarian of British Home Secretaries, was now secure. The 2010's as a result were comparatively much more relaxed over here on civil liberties issues.

The UK as a result avoided repeating the demonstrations that broke out in Amsterdam over the arrests in Slovakia based on what were deemed lifestyle choices that shouldn't have been on the information system.

The UK avoided the headlines punched out by the shocked German magazine that uncovered how travel details of critics of the European Commission were being stored on the Europol database, and that these had been accessed on several occasions by the Belgian Police and relayed to the European Commission's security goons.

The UK avoided the controversy involving the armed Commission bodyguards, and the faux pas when Europol took the lead in breaking down the wrong door during a joint operation.

There is, in short, more confidence in the British Police, as the public understands who it is responsible to. When a British police chief cocks up, heads roll.

There has also been something of a gentle revolution in the criminal justice system.

The Strasbourg Court of Human Rights was never part of the EU, but inspired so many of the cogs of Brussels, including the European Court of Justice at Brussels, and had become wired into the problem. Over 50 years, a court designed to prevent any repeat of the visceral evil of the Thirties and Forties had drifted into becoming a social commentator, and a mechanism for imposing liberal ideology.

The problem was that these interpretations were jerry-built over the heads of anyone responsible to the electorate. Anyone who objected was made anathema, an enemy of reason.

But under the new system in post-2010 Britain at least, the people got to argue the way in which they lived. This started with a great debate over the criminal justice system. It led a set of compromises, mixing education and opportunity for reform for early offenders with some startling ideas about dissuasion. These ranged from limiting TVs in prisons to five channel black and white sets unless earned by good behaviour, down to the massively controversial trial of Perspex 'dis boxes' on high streets (compared by some with bringing back the stocks, though locally popular).

Regardless of where you stood in the argument, it was undeniable that many of these proposals were previously impossible under the old system, which was all Rights and few wrongs, all carrot and no stick.

With the withdrawal of the UK from the European Convention on Human Rights, and its rejoining a handful of months later with new protocols defining what 'basic rights' were to mean, courts in the UK became less fey. The failed fig leaf of the 1998 Human Rights Act was ripped away, and a new Guiding Statement of Basic Principles was drafted. 'Human Rights' stopped being a motor and became an anchor again.

This took the direction of the courts away from those pushed by ambulance-chasers and moved them towards causes of real concern and genuine redress. In other words, society stopped having spectrally-silhouetted rights, and started to be defined by peoples' freedoms.

Not everyone was happy, of course. There were several large law firms that had profited extremely well from taking public money to fight cases that they themselves had identified as ones that should be pursued.

Cause and effect. A foreign national is encouraged to sue the British Government over allegations about British troops overseas. The Government settles out of court to save costs. The law firm gets a large amount of public money, and looks for more ways to interpret abuses of human rights. The Government, or rather the taxpayer, loses ever more money. Some foreign nationals invent cases in order to become fabulously wealthy, expecting to pay no expenses then settle out of court. The people on the front line become more wary about getting on with doing their job. Their job gets harder to do, at risk to their lives. Cause and effect.

It says a great deal that many lawyers, and a number of very senior judges, quietly welcomed the change and got on with interpreting the law in the old fashioned way; as it had been intended when drafted, and still protecting the vulnerable.

# Identity and Immigration

The general public has been touched in many different ways by such power shifts. The individual, whether you prefer to call him a citizen or a subject, has slowly come to reassess his post-Brussels landscape, and the society around him.

This is very true of one particular rusty old hand grenade in the shed.

Back in the EU days, there was a lot of media attention given to the political fallout around immigration and asylum. This was because of an unhealthy combination of several key factors.

In the first place, the Government kept showing itself up as incapable of managing immigration, unlike successful historic migrant economies such as Canada or Australia. It underestimated for instance the number of Eastern European migrants coming to Britain after EU enlargement by a factor of 1000 per cent. The appearance of illegal immigrants working in airports, alongside Gordon Brown's car, and in the Home Office building itself made a very public fool of the department.

Secondly, there was a perception that there were very large numbers of such individuals in the country, partly because the government was self-evidently incapable of providing an exact figure.

Thirdly, it was clear that public services, particularly transport, were already approaching capacity in the South East, and ministers would not admit how the scale of migration would affect future planning.

Fourthly, there was a belief that the legal service

was weighted in favour of those trying to abuse the system, and indeed rewarding some of their solicitors, while disadvantaging those who were genuine asylum seekers in fear for their family's lives.

Fifthly, there were noted cases driven by the European Courts (Strasbourg in the lead) where deportations authorised by the UK courts were halted. Judges ruled that, even if claimants were flown back to a safe part of their home country, they might somehow still be at risk. It didn't help that destinations Brits happily travelled to on holiday were amongst countries barred. Nor that asylum seekers in some cases were clearly travelling a lot further than they needed to in order to reach a safe country. Something was clearly wrong with the British system if Calais was merely a transit point for refugees.

Since the Home Office admitted it was incapable of managing the issue, it increasingly resolved from the late 1990's onwards to drop its opt outs and entangle itself in EU schemes in order to get someone else to fix it. This very Italian approach simply exacerbated the problem. Common policy was owned by no-one. Meanwhile, baroque blueprints emerged for a central-ised EU programme to handle mass migration, based on sharing out the people. This would lead to front-line countries on the routes, particularly Italy, Spain and Greece, together with countries like Germany that in the past took in huge numbers of refugees, expecting tens of thousands more to be sent on for the United Kingdom to look after.

Crucially, the subject meanwhile became a political taboo. If someone raised questions, it was seen by blind-sided columnists as tantamount to raising a lynch mob. But by encouraging silence on the issue, the liberal press across Europe generated the grim and lethal fog needed for the extremists to thrive. Since no-one else was allowed a contrary opinion, thugs with suits and ties could sell themselves as Robin Hoods, the 'lone voice' against an 'elite consensus' that refused to listen to ordinary people.

The break with the EU policy has rescued the UK from this poison.

A massive debate now means that Westminster has emerged from the newsprint shadows of both the Lindsey Refinery and the undeportable criminal. Bilateral agreements with the EU, North America and Australasia have been set up, allowing for workforce mobility to continue, this time without strikes happening over companies supposedly bringing in people based on their passports.

So Peter still works in Florence, and Pietro in the City.

Meanwhile, more broadly, immigration has been streamlined along Canadian lines. People are accepted on a points system, promoting those who add value to the economy and society, based on the needs of a given year. In 2020, top of the nation's skills shortages list – and 20 points – goes to medical professionals, but last year it was forestry workers, and electrical engineers for a major new motorcycle plant. Meanwhile, asylum policy is run openly and efficiently, streamlined but subject to swift judicial review. The age of long worried waits, state-enforced grant-maintained idleness, and endless indecision over claimants is over.

The net result is that racial tension and political extremism is on the decline in Britain. But sadly, other countries within the EU have yet to learn the lesson.

# The City Trader

Pietro Gallo works in the City. An Italian by birth, he has worked at *Holstein-Morben* for the past three years, living proof that even outside of the old EU structures, the City continues to thrive under a cosmopolitan cloak.

More than that, it thrives because of the way it is treated.

It's hard for most people to get a feel of the importance of the place. The image is one of pin stripes and braces, of lunar glass monoliths, rather than of the management of your pension fund.

This was a dangerous prejudice. The City accounted for just under four per cent of the national GDP. It was a major taxpayer, was a significant contributor to the Balance of Payments, and was a major employer, with around 345,000 people working in the finance and professional support services.

It was also by far the largest financial centre in Europe. While New York's was larger, much of this was internal to the States rather than focused on world markets. As such, London was the true global centre, with more international banking, foreign exchange dealing, trading in international equities, international bond issuance, and international bond trading than any other location. It was also the world's leading market for international insurance.

Under the EU, the financial markets were too often seen by continental politicians as subject matter for one of two portraits. Either it was a gigantic rubber tree, waiting to be tapped, slave drained of an unending supply of sap and, as long as the juice kept flowing, whose browning leaves were to be ignored.

Or they were a Bosch landscape of Beelzebub's playthings, an untrammelled Anglo-Saxon banking hell whose denizens deserved due damnation.

Either way, the City was the key hub of the perfidious world banking system that lay within the reach of the EU regulators. As a direct consequence, it suffered.

The Financial Services Action Plan (FSAP) inflicted heavy compliance costs on financial services firms, through a barrage of 40 expensive harmonising measures.

The Markets in Financial Instruments Directive (MiFID) inflicted perhaps three quarters of the whole EU compliance and IT costs on the UK alone, an estimated £6.5 billion, adding barriers for new firms and hamstringing new competition. The Capital Requirements Directive added another £7 billion costs in the UK, making the UK markets less competitive than their New York counterparts.

The Consumer Credit Directive reduced access to finance and increased the cost of credit. The Distance Marketing Directive added costs in a poorly drafted text that had no clear benefit. The Insurance Mediation Directive added another £400 million annual costs, passed onto the consumers. The Payment Services Directive required banks to massively reorganise their infrastructure, at a cost across Europe of £8.6 billion.

The list, alien to most of us, ran to reams. The Insurance Mediation Directive, the Distance Marketing Directive, and the Market Abuse Directive.

The Transparency Directive, the Prospectus Directive, and the Takeovers Directive. The Hedge Fund Directive, and the Systemic Risk Board.

The state of play is easier to understand if we take a pace back and look at the trading of an easier commodity to picture.

Artists' Resale Right, or *Droit de Suite*, was a principle founded on good intent. European legislators, especially the French, were mindful that many famous great artists had not profited from their fame while alive. Vermeer and Van Gogh were not alone in dying poor, while their paintings in contrast generated huge profits for future dealers. The idea was therefore to create a tax that might be levied, so that a percentage of the trade could be passed on to their descendents.

As it happened, the revenue collected initially proved relatively small, albeit still bitterly felt (especially the paperwork) by the smaller dealers. The Treasury had been prodded into action, and had put in derogations that softened the initial blow. But then in 2010, the costs increased fourfold, and the evidence became more marked.

While not disastrous, it provided a microcosm of how well-meaning regulations had a universal impact, even when just a single one was applied and not a layer.

The problem was that this law was unilateral. Art houses within the EU – the biggest were in London – would have to pay the levy, passing on the extra cost to the person selling the artwork. Their competitors in Geneva and New York would not.

This meant that art sellers would find it more profitable to sell the art work outside the EU, and would choose to do so, which in turn incidentally still meant that money wouldn't go to the artists' relatives.

Business would be driven outside of the EU, and the only net effect was that London trade suffered.

That was also the problem with EU regulation and the City in a nutshell, and it was exacerbated by the fact that a number of governments willingly engaged in such shenanigans hoping that by hobbling London, their own financial centres would profit. It was, frankly, not very *communautaire*, and alone knifed the idea that EU membership was one huge noble cause.

It was an arrangement London got out of in the nick of time. The Chairman of the Committee that regulated the European Securities had already declared that harmonisation was "moving ahead at full steam", with a move for a centrally-controlled system aimed to be up and running by the close of 2010. In this and other new structures, the UK representative was set to find himself with the same voting power as Malta, despite representing the financial powerhouse of the continent.

The consequences were obvious: regulations made that were damaging to countries that weren't in the Euro, that were opposed to red tape, or were simply too successful in comparison with their European competitors. London ticked all three boxes.

New projects now included the creation of a European Systemic Risk Council (ESRC) and a European System of Financial Supervision (ESFS). The ESRC was designed as a big picture supervisor and adviser.

The ESFS on the other hand would lead to the establishment of European Supervisory Authorities (ESAs) overseeing banking, insurance and securities. They would have a range of legally binding powers, with the European Court of Justice given the role of supreme arbiter.

The problem was not that rules were not needed. The collapse of the financial markets amply and dismally demonstrated that procedures were either not in place, or were not being followed. The problem was that the solution attacked the walnut with acid.

National supervisors were set to have their authority undermined. The use of Qualified Majority Voting allowed for rules to be passed that were not in the interests of the UK's Financial Services Authority, or the UK economy. A liability gap was now emerging that looked dangerously set to ensnare British taxpayers in future financial crises. Liability for future failures looked uncertain. Day-to-day management of banks looked set to shift out of national control. The European Central Bank – with very limited UK representation – would take the central managerial role.

All this on a shaky legal basis! The only article used as the legal bedrock was Article 95, quoted when there was nothing in the treaties that actually allowed the European Communities to carry out an action, but where governments agreed to go ahead in support of the Single Market all the same. It was the diplomatic form of dodgy accounting.

Holstein-Morben's head office finds this all too familiar. Miracle of miracles, the removal of London's financial markets from the EU's grasp in 2010 slowed down the urge in Brussels to forge so many shackles. London, as the key competitor of Paris, Madrid and Frankfurt, would no longer after all be the prime victim, but their own markets. But enough trip wires and mantraps remained for players by the Seine and on the Main to find it more rewarding to shift much of their operations into the freer, blue water territories of the London regulators. It was either there, or to Zurich, Tokyo or Manhattan.

Brussels hadn't yet killed the goose that laid the golden egg, but in 2020 the hands are still firmly locked around its throat.

# Part Two: "Events, Dear Boy, Events"

## History in a Nutshell

*Errant Footfall*

It has been a decade now since the UK resolved to go its own way. Ten years on, in 2020, the scale of the event has today slipped into the alcoves of the public's consciousness. Pub talk as ever is focused on reality telly and modern controversy, not least the latest attempt by a foreign court to extradite the Earl of Sedgefield over those distant decisions that led to Basrah and Baghdad.

Yet this year has seen minds refocusing. The tenth anniversary of Britain's historic decision reunited for one final day-long television special the old 'Triple S' billing of Professors Schama, Starkey and Snow. Their swansong historical review covered with some skill a half century of what some TV guide writers had feared might prove to be "boredom on a stick" and little more than "five hours of monologue on the relative merits of standardising tractor parts". In the event, though, it proved something of a hit – perhaps helped by recent revelations from the Kew archives, and skilful computer graphics reincarnating some of the players from the past, even if this occasion proved bereft of fancy jewel-decked costumes, and tanks in a simulated sand pit.

Further afield over the week, some of the old guard presided over a handful of public events: a string of country galas; a conference in Cardiff's City Hall, chosen as a previous EU summit site; even an obligatory day trip to Bruges by a tanked up band of cross-dressing students armed with handbags, which the Flemish Press saw the funny side of even if Lille's Eurostar gendarmerie did not.

But no fireworks. The commemoration was strangely British in that regard.

Perhaps the format was most appropriate because of the very way in which this revolution had itself taken place; a gentle, almost surprising overthrow rather than one of gunpowder and chaos.

Few had seen the warning signs, though they had been in plain view. Of itself, that fact spoke too eloquently about the fundamental flaw in the European project. From a British perspective, the politics of 2009 was increasingly and almost obsessively focused on a single vanishing point. As in the dog end days of the John Major government, the question invariably being asked was *when?*

*When* would Brown call the General Election? *When* would backbench Labour MPs start to get the jitters again about their crumbling prospects for re-election? *When* would the next scandal break? *When* would someone in the Labour Party decide to stake a last throw of the dice at being a Prime Minister for a season, instead of mutely accepting the nugatory promise of ending a career as a failed Leader of the Opposition?

The Prime Minister had lost control of the

Government, and the Government of the agenda. In short, by the second half of 2009, the brakes fell off and pretty well with them, the wheels. The overwhelming centre of press attention was the looming brick wall and the inevitable impact, the sickening spark-specked slow motion of the anticipated accident. The focus was absolute and overbearing. The peripheral was easily missed.

### Ask and Ask Again

Curiously interlinked with this lunchtime soap script was the ongoing saga of the EU Constitution. The prospect of a new government in Whitehall galvanised those outside Britain who fought on against the Lisbon Treaty. By now, of course, the supposed 'show stoppers' of the failed Dutch and French referenda had been penny conjured away by the simple expedient of ignoring the votes and pretending they didn't apply to the text now in hand.

The people had spoken. But the elite plugged their fingers in their ears.

The Irish had proved a different proposition. Their referendum was a constitutional stop sign. It couldn't be driven round, only smashed over. Months of prevarication failed to provide inspiration for the Yesmongers; sombre smoke-fogged evenings failed to deliver the genius of a poetic compromise worthy of Dublin's old wordsmiths that would carry the people along with them.

Happily for the integrationists, if no-one else, a world banking crisis thundered into the field. When, in autumn 2009, the Irish were dragged to the polls once again, the deck had been reshuffled. Ireland, the voters were told, had to vote Yes because otherwise the next financial and housing crisis would drag them under. The country wasn't 'big enough' to survive on its own. If they didn't muck in with their fellow Europeans, if they didn't show some *gratitude* for all the alms and gold that had so generously been cast at the Emerald Isle for the past few decades, then they would be dumped back onto the verges of the B road of history, pig under the arm and waiting for Godot.

The threat was bleak, raw, crude, naïve and vicious. But as it came with the Irish Government's blessing, backed up by a panoply of guest star visitors from chanceries across Europe, their sins went unpunished.

Declan Ganley's wunderkind machine had predictably run out of diesel after his ill-starred decision to run in the Euro elections as *Libertas*. His absence for most of the campaign proved a gift to the Yes camp. That still left a seasoned group of Nay sayers, veterans of past campaigns, whose arguments had clearly not tarnished with time. But several months of high level leverage on senior Church figures through the EU-funded COMECE had also taken its effect. Although in the main the hierarchy upheld its neutrality, a couple of bishops had provided sufficient equivocal support to the Yes side to hint that St Peter's Keys might also unlock the gates of Lisbon. Then there was the funding. The No campaign, dependent upon donations from ordinary citizens, had already exhausted its finances in the last round.

The Yes camp, meanwhile, had already seen its acolytes earmarked for hundreds of thousands of Euros of support in "information grants". The public, it was said, needed to be more 'informed' on the constitutional treaty, more 'educated'. So money poured out of the main MEP slush funds; sluiced out of the budgets run from the Commission; gushed from the business and union lobbies also being kept afloat by EU subventions. The airwaves and print were bought, and the pens of editors followed.

The cream proved to be the adherence of a handful of rock stars, poets and TV celebs co-opted for a day. A day proved enough. Despite an unfaulted campaign fired with national spirit, the No side could not keep standing, and buckled under a barrage that spoke more of the bullying perpetrator than of the endurance of the victim, in this case Irish democracy.

The parties ran on late into the night down Ixelles way, and few Brussels stagiaires paid heed beyond their champagne glasses of the very mixed reactions of the bar staff at *O'Reilly's*, *Kitty O'Shea's* and the *James Joyce*. Meanwhile, the lights were burning in the capitals of Eastern Europe.

### Eastward Ho!

The Czechs and Poles were to be next. With a brief hiccough from the German constitutional court dealt with, pressure now mounted on the respective presidents to ratify the treaty. The Poles would not stand alone; it depended upon Prague's President, the redoubtable Václav Klaus.

Klaus's position was a longstanding one. He had viewed joining the EU as an economic necessity, since two thirds of Czech foreign trade was with the EU. Of that, two thirds with Germany alone, and since 1973 there had not been any real EFTA alternative on offer. But trade was one thing, integration was quite another; and his understanding of the treaty (especially the mechanism for future ratifications) led him to realise he was the man at the brakes at the last point before the incline meant ever-closer union became unstoppable.

He also saw the construct as fundamentally flawed. As he had put it before the European Parliament, on the occasion when MEPs jeered him for criticising an unwillingness to listen to other viewpoints,

"When I said that European Union membership did not have and does not have any alternative, I only mentioned half of what must be said. The other – logical – half of my statement is that the methods and forms of European integration do, on the contrary, have quite a number of possible and legitimate variants, just as they proved to have in the last half century. There is no end of history. Claiming that the status quo, the present institutional form of the EU, is a forever uncriticizable dogma, is a mistake that has been – unfortunately – rapidly spreading, even though it is in direct contradiction not only with rational thinking but also with the whole two-thousand-year history of European civilization."

He continued with an example of modern political farce,

"Many of you certainly know the name of the French economist Frederic Bastiat and his famous

Petition of the Candlemakers, which has become a well-known and canonical reading illustrating the absurdity of political intervention in the economy. On 14 November 2008 the European Commission approved a real, not a fictitious Bastiat's Petition of the Candlemakers and imposed a 66% tariff on candles imported from China. I would have never believed that a 160-year-old essay could become reality, but it has happened. An inevitable effect of the extensive implementation of such measures in Europe is economic slowdown, if not a complete halt of economic growth. The only solution is liberalisation and deregulation of the European economy."

Such views were to a great extent shared by the Polish administration, which also had yet to ratify the Treaty. They were less popular in Brussels. Pressure now built up, directly on the Presidency as well as through proxies in Prague, including the threat of impeachment. Spokesmen for campaign groups emerged from Ostrava to Děčín claiming that the President was being 'unreasonable', 'confrontational', even 'unconstitutional'. Students protested; lawyers wrote letters; judges penned articles; political youth groups challenged MPs; charities warned of the end of essential grants; MEPs threatened their compatriots with dire isolation; business leaders and union chiefs invented job losses; indoctrinated journalists reported all of it.

Too many of these front men for the treaty shared one thing in common; they had been moulded by years of EU funding, the infamous old B3 budget lines for civic society and students. The Danegeld had been paid, stipends and scholarships, hotlines and chauffeurs, and there was always the prospect of more.

Even before the result of the Irish referendum was publicly announced, senior anti-treaty politicians across the continent had already been urging the Czech governing party to hold out. In a few months' time, there would be a General Election in the United Kingdom; the polls indicated a Conservative victory; Conservative policy was to have a referendum before ratifying, carrying the powerful prospect of a No vote. Those who opposed the wretched treaty just had to fight for time. "You will be like the Spartans at Thermopylae", had observed the MP and veteran ally David Heathcoat-Amory. "You can hold the pass while the rest of civilisation rallies and comes on to victory."

"There is only one problem with that," rejoined the Czech. "The Spartans died."

### Selling the Pass

It was here that a critical strategic mistake was made.

While many followed Mr Heathcoat-Amory's lead and openly supported the Czech President's stand, the Tory Party leadership only gave support from the shadows.

Had David Cameron or William Hague publicly called upon Klaus to pause for the British people to express its opinion, an opportunity denied to so many across the continent, things might have turned out differently.

A rallying pennant would have been lifted on the field. The Czechs could have mustered around another democratic reality, replacing the self-bound constraint of the Irish referendum with a British one. The charge of the Treaty forces would have lost its impetus, and politicians would have had to retreat to the abandoned pledge of doing less and doing it better. The negotiating position of the Eurosceptic premiers in the new Intergovernmental Conference meanwhile would have been institutionally vastly stronger. *One false move*, as it were, *and the Lisbon Treaty gets it*. It would have made reaching a new arrangement considerably easier.

But it is a moot point.

Senior political advisers to the Tories decided that they could not contemplate doing what every other capital city in Europe was already engaged in; telling the Czechs how to run their domestic politics. Some saw it as an argument that might make too many enemies on *Newsnight* and fire up similar lobbyists back home. Others looked at the division amongst Czech politicians and feared similar splits closer to home. Some were non-believers, others just preferred to skirt trouble, bystanders to principle.

For want of a nail the kingdom was lost. Warsaw swiftly buckled. Without official support from the likely future British Government, the Czechs were isolated and forced to concede. The last of the dominoes was forced down with a clatter. Conservative policy was in rags.

Renegotiating the deal over Lisbon would now be an exclusively British problem.

The sad irony was that all this happened as the New Labour endgame was in sight. Gordon Brown's electoral seepage had continued without stop. Newspaper cartoonists pictured him as the skipper of an electoral Exxon Valdez, or sketched him as a nail-gnawing alien from the new movie *Planet 51*.

It was a John Major scenario, though one that ended with a magnesium flare up. The trigger, of all things, was an article in the *New Statesman*.

A redbrick university political scientist published an analysis of the projected wipeout of the Labour back benches, and then coupled this with a spoof algorithm to calculate the mathematical probability of another leadership challenge, what became known as the "Kirkcaldy Tipping Point";

$$l = S \frac{tr}{c} + \frac{1}{v} + \frac{p}{a} + \frac{(f1)}{(f2)} + \frac{01}{02} - e^2$$

Where $l$ is loyalty, $S$ the current ministerial salary, $t$ the time remaining to profit from a minister's generous pay packet, $r$ the elder statesman rank achievable before the election, $c$ the prospect of advancement after a coup, $v$ the time left to settle old scores by knifing colleagues, $p$ pension rights that might be lost, $a$ personal ambition, $f1$ fear of the loss of the seat being accelerated by an early election, and $f2$ the current fear of the loss of the seat, $O1$ the MP's age over 60, and $O2$ under 50 when imagining a number of years in Opposition, and $e$ the number of vacant peerages left that the wobbler might be bought off with.

In other words, with ministers increasingly panicking the variable turned into a certainty the nearer the election got. The feedback from befuddled *Newsnight* audiences was that the algebra was only marginally more understandable than an Open University lecture after four pints of Kronenbourg, but it started MPs thinking, and after that, plotting. Not that by this stage they needed too much encouragement.

### End Game

A race now ensued between Caesar and Brutus. The Prime Minister's remaining inner cabal was by now restricted to old hands destined for retirement, or damaged goods such as Tory defectors with no other warlord to adhere to. These pushed for a Götterdämmerung election before the leadership could be challenged. Racing against them were the political assassins of the upcoming Labour generation such as Burnham and Flint. In the absence of a Granita deal, a Strangers' Bar one had to do, with Blears backing Johnson in what the press cruelly jibed as the Flotsam and Jetsam pact, under the benevolent gaze of "Tonton Reid".

The putsch gave the Conservatives a run for their money, and seeded one last astonishing flowering of Labour policy – watered from the hidden wells of Frank Field and Bob Marshall-Andrews, since the usual streams by now had long been sucked dry or lay in drought.

Medicash, including proposals for community rather than individual cover.

A Public Sector Reform bill, which shifted super-salaries for state employees towards performance-driven pay, ended guarantees of a fixed percentage of the civil service receiving bonuses, and stopped promoting people out of failure.

Public Honours reform, restoring the original meaning to both words in the term.

A complete overthrow of the bureaucratic targets system, in return for a fig-leaf pledge of 'best intent'.

The end of 42 days' detention, with the declaration that the immediate 9/11 and 7/7 crisis had passed.

A review of criminal legislation, repealing those that had been little used by the police.

An end to state pensions for all future school leavers – of all things, an old Peter Lilley policy lifted from Singapore, over which Labour back in 1997 had fuelled a panic amongst pensioners by saying it applied to current OAPs.

Yet more socialist 'windfall' taxes on oil companies and airlines, but hypothecated on renewables research, to establish the UK as the leading world manufacturer of solar cells and micro-generation in anticipation of international Green hysteria.

Charities reform, cutting superstar wages for cliques paid out of charitable donations.

Even simple public gestures such as sending, on a rotational basis, a Government minister or his PPS to Brize Norton for each repatriation ceremony.

Some of these ideas would indeed be taken up in the coming Parliament. But the revolution came too late for the Labour leadership to be the proposing ministers. By 2010, the tag line of "thirteen lost years", combined with adverts showing quotes about "no more boom and bust" superimposed on that now famous street with all the repossessions, hit the mark. The ambush of the PM by the sacked village post master, and the Lib Dem press meeting held in an abandoned Woolworths store, proved a little close to the bone. (The less said about that minor party's *liar, liar pants on fire* stunt, by far the better.)

The vote was tighter than had been expected for the previous two years, but still clear and conclusive. David Cameron found the official car waiting for him outside Millbank ready to leave for the Palace, and his first day in office began.

His in tray was famously 'overhanging', almost as shocking as the nuclear weapons induction film. The top third of the files hillock related to the scale of public debt his team had inherited. One packed red box provided a summary of the PFI and PPP figures that Government had been sitting on for the past decade. The figures were frightening; of course they would utterly dominate the opening weeks in office, and loom over the following months as well.

Then there were the election pledges that had been made for the first week in government. The one that had caught the public imagination was the massive quango cull, and the tabloids took great delight in following the major gardening exercise that hacked away at so much dead wood, particularly where one careerist quangonaut was caught out trying to claim for compensation for no longer sitting on two particularly ropey committees in subjects where she was patently unqualified.

The other dominant media story was the big picture policy line up. Initially, the press focused on the 'Great Education Reform Bill', actually a series of individually unconnected proposals affecting university degree standards, A and GCSE level grading, the O level option, devolving choice to Councils over reverting to the 11 Plus, deregulating apprenticeships, and funding management. Although only one element of the policy package, this proved to be the real enduring manifesto legacy of the first term in government.

At this stage, Brussels barely featured on the agenda. There had been a few reports on issues relating to the horizon-spanning EU tax, VAT, taking in Bingo, church roofs, and the perennial threat to tax newspapers, books and children's clothes. The campaign against the tax on suncream faded with the weather. It was actually the ongoing digitalisation of television that emerged as the first EU news blip. Anecdotal evidence was now coming out about difficulties with disposing of the old TV sets. Millions were being dumped, or traded in for new ones. But under the Waste Electrical and Electronic Equipment (WEEE) Directive, there was a heavy obligation to recycle; under the landfill directive there was a limit to dumping; and further regulations limited the landfill permitted for island communities. The road to this particular analogue Hell was paved with good intentions, but ended up all the same as a rerun of the fridge mountain fiasco. An interrupted shipment to India, and the £30 million bill to date, put EU regulations briefly in the news.

### An Accident Waiting to Happen

Historians tend to step back and put the negotiations into a broader context, seeing the developments of

2010 as a self-inflicted wound by European integrationists. The events that led to the UK and others to break with the old core of the EU were utterly avoidable. Ambition overcame common sense; ideology overcame reason; the abstract overcame the democratic.

Things could have turned out all so differently. It all boiled down to a meeting in Brussels one December, nine years before.

The EU's leaders had met behind the magnificent gilded gates of a nineteenth century royal palace to the north of Brussels. The venue was Laeken. The place would lend its name to a lost mandate and a massive political betrayal.

The meeting moulded the framework for a great conference that would take place over 2002–3, the Convention on the Future of Europe. Leaders recognised that the EU kept holding referenda and losing them. Clearly, the premiers conceded magnanimously, the people had lost faith in the project. Something had to be done to win them round, even if this meant a move as radical as circumscribing powers already held, or even handing them back.

The Convention met in turn to debate these proposals, and for the first 48 hours all was well. Then the Commission recognised a basic truth. The majority of the delegates, 99 per cent of them political appointees, did not represent the popular opinions that had triggered Laeken in the first place. They were part of the political elite that lay behind the problem. A number were from applicant countries, keen neither to rock the boat nor in some cases ruin their own chances of a lucrative new career. Many others were appointed because they knew the Brussels scene, which by definition meant that they had bought into it.

It was as though, after the American War of Independence, the members of the Philadelphia Convention had been shipped in straight from Bristol.

Overnight, on the Thursday of the first week, the Commission changed tack and ceased talking about what powers would be handed back. Meanwhile, the membership of the dominant body in the Convention had been settled. The Praesidium would be headed by a French federalist, with an Italian and a Belgian federalist as his deputy, and a British Foreign Office mandarin heading up the secretariat who was, well, less than entirely convincing as an advocate of the minority position. As this was the body that prepared the key treaty drafts, the end fate of the Convention was now predestined. What had been referred to at Laeken as a possible Constitution down the line and seen as just one future option, had become the *sine qua non* of a body of men – Giscard d'Estaing foremost amongst them – who saw themselves as Europe's new founding fathers, with a mandate and a mission to match.

The actual Laeken mandate and the end result were so markedly different.

Laeken described the Union as *"behaving too bureaucratically"*, yet the draft Constitution failed to address the then-102,000 pages of the acquis communautaire, and proposed a new legal instrument, the 'Non Legislative Act', whereby the Commission could pass binding laws.

Laeken said *"the Union must be brought closer to its citizens"*. But the transfer of more decision making from member states to the Union, concerning criminal justice matters and new areas of domestic policy, made the Union more remote.

Laeken added that *"the division of competences be made more transparent"*. But the new category of 'shared competences' gave no assurance about how power was to be shared, particularly as member states would be forbidden to legislate in these areas if the Union decided to act.

Laeken called for the *"European institutions to be less unwieldy and rigid"*. But the Constitution gave more power to all the existing EU institutions and created a Europe of Presidents, including a new Eurozone Presidency, with more jobs for politicians and less influence for the people.

Laeken highlighted the importance of *national parliaments,* and the Nice Treaty *"stressed the need to examine their role in European integration"*. Yet National Parliaments lost influence relative to the Commission and the European Parliament. Their proposed new role in 'ensuring' compliance with the Subsidiarity Principle in reality gave them no more than a right of request which the Commission could ignore, since a proposal granting a veto role had been rejected.

Laeken called for *"more transparency and efficiency"* in the Union. But the Constitution concentrated more executive and budgetary power in the very EU institutions which had been the subject of repeated and continuing scandals over mismanagement, waste and fraud.

Laeken emphasised simplification: *"if we are to have greater transparency, simplification is essential"*. Yet the draft constitution ran to over 200 pages; the Lisbon Treaty which tinkered with it only kept to the promise of being shorter because the font size was changed. The institutional provisions were in reality the result of contorted compromises, and hardly a document of clarity and inspiration.

Laeken's overriding aim was a *Democratic Europe*. Yet the Constitution created a new centralised European state, more powerful, more remote, with more politicians, more bureaucracy, and a wider gap between the rulers and the ruled.

It was the biggest missed opportunity since the Joseph Galloway compromise of 1774 failed by one vote to bring a settlement to the American colonies; or the last time England played in a world cup. It was also the Indian Summer for those projecting alternatives to integration, suggesting different models that according to the mandate should at least have been picked up for study.

### Never Was

One case was a paper on whistleblowers, which took a half dozen case studies of how the system suppressed the reporting of failure, and how those seeking to correct it were treated as dissidents to be crushed. Another was a short appeal by youth from no less than 30 European countries, calling for a Europe of cooperation rather than integration. Fishermen wrote in to explain the realities of the Common Fisheries Policy, and what could be done to fix it.

Delegates to the Council of Europe made the case for more reference to that intergovernmental body. Extraordinarily, senior diplomats and military men warned of the dangers of the EU's Defence and Diplomatic drift.

Then there was the Minority Report, an alternative text actually submitted by delegates to heads of government alongside the EU Constitution, but dropped like a scalding oven tray.

It certainly could not be said that these were reports from an eclectic handful. One submission alone carried the signatures of former Prime Ministers, Opposition Leaders, Cabinet Ministers and Presidential candidates.

It was not through lack of trying on their part, or a dearth of alternate view points, that the other members of the Convention ended up writing an EU Constitution. It was not through a lack of ideas that the various prime ministers ended up signing up to a treaty that offered, as an answer to rejection, more of the same. It was therefore inevitable that the Treaty of Lisbon was in turn pushed with exactly the same cack-handed democratic disdain. From fearing a need for reform, premiers had turned to fear reform itself.

That opportunity, to redeem an EU from the Atlantic to the Urals, would never happen again.

Such had been the backdrop to the five years preceding Cameron's accession to power. The response to these atrocities to democracy seemed bewilderingly mild.

## Do the Maths

The first manifesto commitment had been entered into in 2008, an understated, even ethereal, threat that if Lisbon were ratified, Conservatives "would not let matters rest there". While intended as a policy sticking plaster, as the EU rose back up the political agenda this commitment moved to centre stage.

A second crucial element was a clear cut pledge to restore the Social Chapter opt out, which by definition meant that a renegotiation of the treaties was on the cards.

Much to their surprise, the new Government found that, in an ionised political atmosphere, these commitments began to build their own momentum, carrying it forward to contemplate a more fundamental realignment in ways that even a year earlier it would have thought unimaginable.

The red button was a promise made in late 2009 that had appeared to be little more than a sensible accounting exercise. It was a pledge on entering office just to do the sums. Treasury officials would be quietly instructed within the first week of the new government to begin a cost-benefit analysis of EU membership.

The concept had long been highly controversial. On at least two occasions, previous Chancellors had quashed research looking into the figures. Both Ken Clark and Gordon Brown had pulled the plug on the suspicion that the figures likely to emerge were not going to be very happy ones; in Chancellor Brown's case, the analysis was pooh poohed as a stunt by relatively junior staff on their own initiative.

Treasury staff were tasked with coming up with the basic audit: net and gross budget contributions; cost of red tape; impact on trade with EU member states; tariff barriers with the rest of the world; projected emerging markets, and so on. Other government departments were invited to contribute to the more broad brush aspects in areas relating to them. Civil servants took to the task with fascination and aplomb.

The five pages contributed by the Leader of the House were the most contentious, dealing with the abstracts of democracy and accountability, though the Home Secretary's chapter also sparked some Cabinet controversy in the civil liberties paragraphs.

In any event, the Treasury officials beavered away over the late spring. The initial figures quickly leaked, hardly surprising given the sums involved. The early working draft revealed that there was a division of opinion. One group of civil servants took a laser beam view and held that EU membership cost the UK four per cent of its GDP every year in fees and bills. A second group, however, held that this figure did not reflect accurately the subsidiary and more widespread damaging effects of membership, and held the true figure to run at between 8 and 9 per cent.

The British press were staggered; "Mugged!" bellowed the front page of *The Sun*. The continental press in turn took a particular interest when the figures across the EU as a whole were released. This was originally intended to be kept from the final document for reasons of diplomatic nicety. They ran at €1,219 billion per year. With 500 million EU citizens, that cost an average of nearly €2,500 per EU citizen every year.

Attempts to rubbish the statistics were blown out of the water by former European Commissioner Gunther Verheugen, who was interviewed in bronzed beachfront retirement and restated his former claim that EU red tape alone cost businesses €600 billion, or around a twentieth of the whole EU economy.

The conservative Treasury estimate now looked excessively cautious, and consensus settled at a cost to the UK (depending upon the Pound/Euro exchange rate) running in the order of between £117 billion and £134 billion per year.

Against this, the benefits looked weak. This was because there remained considerable uncertainty as to what tariff and non-tariff barriers UK exporters would face if the country were not a member. The Department of Business had already for some time assessed that even outside of the EU, the UK would still enjoy preferential access. In the worst case scenario this would be the "most favoured nation tariff", a misnomer as this provided for no preferential tariff, though in turn it would itself encourage the UK (and EU exporters as well) to establish a free trade agreement.

The wild card was over non-tariff barriers, particularly differences in regulations, such as Health and Safety rules. The best case scenario was initially viewed as a deal permitting full continuing access to the Single Market similar to that of members of the European Free Trade Area (EFTA), though without influencing the legislation that governed it.

On review, however, that position was struck out as too much a legacy of an old political holding line, designed to distract MPs from possible alternatives.

New choices were explored; a bilateral trading agreement, such as that between the EU and Canada or Mexico, which were 'EEC Treaty Lite'; reinvigorating and expanding EFTA, and re-establishing a broader bilateral deal; or adopting a unilateral *quid pro quo* arrangement so that if legislation hampered UK exports, similar levels of bureaucracy would be placed on EU imports until the situation was fixed.

There were as a result several possible costings as to how trade would be affected in the new post-EU world. The one thing that officials agreed on was that in each case, developing WTO rules had made international trade a very different proposition from the time of the UK's accession to the EEC. World tariff levels had plummeted, so the physical trade benefits of membership had diminished considerably and were outmatched by the costs. The weights in the balance that had encouraged joining the EEC in the 1960s and 1970s, and which until 1976 had still seemed to justify the decision, now greatly tipped the other way.

The officials tallied the costs with the benefits that couldn't be achieved with a bilateral arrangement. They came up with the bill for the political project of building a country called Europe.

All told, membership cost Britain around £100 billion more than it brought in, nine tenths of which were due to the bureaucracy. The remainder came straight out of the till every year.

Britain was paying a premium to belong to a gym that beat it up.

It now became clear why such a report had previously been quashed. Journalists went mental.

MPs were outraged. Taxpayers were flabber-gasted. The call had already gone out for a new Fontainebleau deal. Many started to demand some-thing far more radical; a couple of billion in rebate this time was not going to wash.

## Forearmed

The timing for this explosion was fortuitous. Before the General Election, David Cameron had already made a pledge to renegotiate certain parts of the treaty.

This was not as radical as it had appeared. Back in 2009, before the Lisbon Treaty was finally ratified, the treaties were still in the process of change and negotiation, as witnessed by the wispy pledges made to sweeten the pill to the Irish.

The Conservatives' key areas for discussion were carefully spelled out, starting with restoring the Social Chapter opt out. That had been effortlessly surrendered as a token during New Labour's first meeting of EU Ministers in 1997, giving up a hard fought compromise without getting anything in return.

However, the responsible ministers were not quite sure if they were mandated to go to the wall over the fisheries debacle or the scandalous running of the EU development funds. Negotiating without the menace of blocking Lisbon had weakened Cameron's hand, and turned him into the representative of one single government amongst twenty seven.

The emergence of the cost figures behind EU membership now rescued the Prime Minister from a damaging and unedifying compromise. It gave him a popular mandate and secured an outspoken parliamentary majority. He was onto a winner. If he got the deal, he came away with the powers. If he didn't, he came away with the money.

The Foreign Secretary was correspondingly sent on the first of his shuttle runs to Brussels and beyond. Rather than a back-of-an-envelope list appropriate for a cornershop foray, his team turned to established and more serious drafts. The rich tradition of British Euroscepticism had long laid the groundwork.

The dossier's demands were logical and straightforward.

It required all aspects of foreign and defence policy to revert to intergovernmental agreement where it involved the UK.

It provided for the protection of the UK's separate legal and judicial system, since the UK would opt out of all elements of the new Treaty that brought Justice and Home Affairs into EU competence.

It restored legislative and regulatory authority to the UK Parliament, so that no new EU legislation would have effect in the UK unless specific legislation was introduced and passed by MPs, and the UK could not be forced to adopt such laws.

The UK Parliament would also have unfettered power to repeal existing EU regulations.

It was further noted that the European Court of Justice had itself become an engine of integration. Correspondingly, the ECJ would be unable to rule on any matter where Parliament had passed a law which conflicted with EU law. British judges would have the final say.

The ability to opt in or out of specific EU programmes was also stated, adjusting Britain's budget contribution to reflect whether or not it participated. The list of opt-out programmes included the CAP, Fisheries, and various initiatives that teetered on Euro-propaganda. It was recognised that the British Government might be willing to continue to engage in areas such as the environment, transport networks and cross border security – although since these would be subject to the condition that no regulations could take effect in the UK unless passed by Parliament, they would essentially become intergovernmental so far as the UK was concerned.

Another key element related to Britain's position towards the Single Market, addressing tariffs and trade policy. While firmly committed to maintaining a free trade area in Europe, and generally seeking to reach a common European negotiating position in external trade negotiations, the UK would reserve the right to take a separate position and negotiate separate agreements if we thought it necessary to do so. In those instances, we could sign up to agreements and bilateral deals that better suited our own needs.

However, and most crucially, it was recognised that the Single Market had already wandered into the realm of protectionism. Contrary to its founding ideals, focus was increasingly on passing laws to regulate "level playing fields". Competition was outlawed as being "unfair", dragging competitiveness within the EU down to the level of the least competent, to the sole benefit of foreign competitors. To complete the football analogy, two teams of hamstrung players were all now kicking the ball uphill. The new arrangement would at least give the British side the choice of their half of the pitch.

Free movement of goods, services and capital meanwhile would still be upheld, though with a reserve on free movement of labour that allowed the Government to intervene to curtail high volumes of migration.

It was, in effect, a series of proposals to allow the United Kingdom to trade in the EU, while stepping away from the political integration. It was a permanent solution to an intractable fifty year old problem: *"Que faire avec ces maudits Anglais?"*

The demands were negotiable, at least initially. The outcry at the revelation of the true costs of membership implanted a backbone into the Foreign Office; a number of the relevent vertebrae were directly transplanted from some Treasury officials who had seen the books being cooked for so long that they revolted over the stew.

## Una Paloma Blanca

The Lisbon Treaty had introduced a permanent Council President. Rather ironically, this British innovation somewhat hampered initial negotiations because of a now rather celebrated personality clash with the new incumbent.

The old system of a rotating presidency still applied to many of the other council areas. The Spanish headed up the Troika holding the remaining powers of the Presidency. This provided an inauspicious start. Madrid remained a major recipient of EU grants; the UK remained the second largest budget contributor;

and it was not in the Iberian interest to surrender this advantage. Moreover, Spanish fleets profited considerably from the Common Fisheries Policy, an area very much directly under threat.

Consequently, there was no movement in the opening weeks of Cameron's premiership.

The tempo changed by July when the Belgians took over at the Troika fore. Although even more ideologically unsympathetic than Madrid, Brussels remained gripped in a political spasm, torn between Left and Right, Flanders and Wallonia, federalism and separatism, België and Belgique. Moreover, with Hungary as the third Troika partner, and Poland set to replace Spain next, the anti-nation state lobby predicted a narrow window of opportunity to limit the damage caused by renegotiation.

### Lobby Fodder

Autumn 2010 saw some rough tackling on the pitch. The Council Presidency, European Parliament majority, and DG Culture separately authorised information expenditure in the old Dublin style. Around two million Euros was earmarked for rapid spending on English language adverts commemorating "the triumph of Europe", and in particular celebrating the fiftieth anniversary of the independence of Nigeria and much of French West Africa; the seventy fifth anniversary of the announcement of German rearmament; and the hundredth of the (relatively deregulated) construction of the *Titanic*. The warehouses of the Union also started to be filled with a dazzling array of inappropriate Europeana; fair trade chocolate bars overprinted with figures about development aid; tea towels showing the 27 member states and the applicants; blue and yellow memory sticks; posters designed for public lavatory walls; Bully the cuddly EU children's toy. These freebies would soon be shipped to the front line.

That was not all. A stream of conferences converged on the British Isles, reminding scientists, journalists, academics, and sundry other beneficiaries of grants, about the wonders offered by uniting together in European Union.

However, DG Communications overplayed its hand. The middle-ranking official putting together one of the schools booklets had not been in post at the time of the infamous *Raspberry Ice Cream War* debacle, when a children's cartoon pamphlet had too blatantly propagandised at the vulnerable. 20,000 copies of a brand new pamphlet, entitled *At the Heart of Europe*, had to be hurriedly pulped when the *Daily Express* ran a front page scoop at what it styled the "Goebbels machine in the playground". Although some criticised the tone of the article, it was clear that the text (which included exhortations to "tell your family about how important peace is for our future", and endorsed biometric identity cards) contravened Section 409 of the Education Act 1996. It didn't help the cause that the spokesman who answered the initial criticisms turned out to be a throaty and barely comprehensible Finn, whose preferred second language was actually German.

Many voices were meanwhile being raised in the business community on both sides of the argument. An overwhelming proportion of small business was outspoken in favour of drastic action. This was hardly surprising; these bore the brunt of the regulations, while enjoying comparatively little feed into the Brussels legislative machine. The Federation of Small Businesses and Forum of Private Business were vociferous partisans of a major shake up. The Chambers of Commerce split, often regionally. The IoD also divided, this time between much of the membership and some of its less critical leadership. The CBI, whose views of European Politics had shown a dubious track record since the 1930s, officially backed a cautious review of red tape, but here again the membership was divided and on the whole more radical than the leadership.

As a rule of thumb, the bigger the business, and the less personally attached the senior management were to the company, the more likely the big bosses were to sign up to the *Keep Britain in Europe* campaign. In some eyes, it made good business sense. Really big businesses were more likely to be kept in the loop in corporatist Brussels, invited into the decision making process, and treated as confidants and co-conspirers. It was hardly surprising that so many of those who participated in the various Brussels meetings of the many business lobby groups should lend their names to a letter to the pro-EU *Financial Times*. It was equally inevitable that within 48 hours their credibility as impartial commentators would be so massively shot to bits, and that shareholders were being invited to tell them to 'step away from the 12 starred podium'. Nevertheless, thanks to some quiet lobbying by certain former Commissioners active in the business community, a series of sizeable cheques continued to flutter in the direction of the Stay Put camp.

In part, this stance was helped by the attitude of the BBC. Hinted opinions featured more than guarded neutrality, varying from Peter Snow to Jeremy Clarkson with a major gap around the middle. It took a long time for presenters to tackle the realities rather than focusing on news balloons floated from the Commission.

The United States Government had historically been the other wild card. Historians cast their minds back to the American Committee for a United Europe (ACUE), an organisation run by WW2 OSS types that had funded European federalists back in the 1950s; they also recalled the reports of direct CIA involvement in the 1975 referendum, which emerged when two agents at the London Station refused to play along and broke cover. This time, however, that camp stayed neutral. There was after all no Soviet Bloc to manoeuvre against. Their counterparts by the Thames, following the Owen Doctrine of the late 1970s, this time did likewise.

The British Government took advantage of the moment. They had promised in the past a referendum on Lisbon. The policy was of key national importance. The opposition was disunited. They therefore called a snap plebiscite. *Do you approve of the British Government's decision to renegotiate its terms of membership of the European Union? Yes or No.* Ministers explained in interviews that a *No* response would mean quietly accepting the Lisbon Treaty, while a *Yes* would provide a mandate to explore the return of powers already ceded. The end result would be approved by Parliament.

Six weeks later, the Yes vote came in, 64.7 per cent to 35.2. Every region, including the most pro-EU regions, London and Scotland, answered in the affirmative.

It was a masterstroke. While opponents attacked it as a blank script, they were also pinioned by their own past mantrap argument that a sovereign Parliament didn't need referenda to make treaties happen. The vote wrong-footed opponents who had intended to focus on narrow specifics in a TV campaign a year down the line, and it gave a fillip to public broadcasters who had been uneasy with unbalanced editorials from their bosses.

The reaction across the Channel was mixed. The Lisbon Treaty had already been passed into law. The text provided for ever-closer union by the back door. By and large, the problems of endless failed referenda – the Neverendums – had now been bypassed. But realists saw that Britain, and a handful of other states, could still continue to keep progress in leg irons, slowing federalism down long enough so that the laurels passed to the next generation. Continental political vistas remained fogged over, and the engine stay in second gear. The destiny remained certain, but the timetable needed to be fixed. Perhaps it was best to settle the future of these agnostic partners now.

Then again, some of the countries with most to lose financially preferred to dally, and in the council meetings that discussed the negotiations (from which the UK was excluded) pushed a policy of lethargy. Time would weaken the British hand, they argued.

But time cut both ways. The fortnightly British

financial transfer to the Communities' coffers was delayed, going through five minutes before the close of the day. The message was clear: do a deal or literally pay the price.

Chastened now by the realisation that the British Government could no longer be shunted aside from its intent, the Council President drew a new conclusion, and returned to the strategic view that had been boxed and left in the policy attic for the past nine years. It was time to look at where Brussels failed.

This viewpoint was reinforced by visits by some extraordinarily serious-looking characters in grey suits. Business leaders from the Rhineland's automobile and chemicals industries paid discreet visits to the top floor of the Berlaymont. *El Pais* and *La Stampa* had been suggesting that a trade war with the recalcitrant British might be in order. Mindful that the UK ran a £3 billion monthly deficit with the EU, these businessmen to the contrary warned bleakly that any trade war would hammer the continent, and their own companies in particular, since it was they who were in the black with their exports. Talk of encouraging three million UK job losses insanely ignored the four million EU jobs that depended on exporting back across the Channel. A trade war would be catastrophic and, they hinted, political suicide.

The British Government also suggested that if other countries tried to hold up proceedings using Lisbon's two year moratorium for member states leaving the EU, London itself was quite capable of playing the same rough game. International law was on its side. It boiled down to the text of a treaty about treaties.

Under article 49 of the Vienna Convention on Treaties, it was possible to argue that after the events of the previous few years, the Lisbon Treaty had only been passed by the fraudulent conduct of several states. As such, the UK could legitimately consider itself able to abrogate the EU treaties overnight, rather than under the terms set out in Lisbon. Moreover, contrary to Article 51 at least two countries had been subject to forms of coercion, and that doubly invalidated it. It was an elegant but obvious diplomatic revolver that sat quietly on the negotiating table, a Mississippi paddleboat card player's guarantee of fair play.

Article 50 was wisely left unexplored. That would have carried the suggestion that several prime ministers had signed away their country's birthrights in the expectation that they themselves would be in the running for a plum new Eurojob.

A deadline was set to sort out the new deal. But William Hague also played up the positives; Britain's role as a world power in its own right that Brussels could cooperate with; the role of the City of London if only it were left unfettered by reactionary legislation; its historical global links; a major trading partner ranking still amongst the most important in the world. With a flattering and self-deprecating twist, behind closed doors he poured in honey to the mix, recalling the comparison of how the United States relied heavily on Canada as a motor of its markets.

Gridlock remained over the detail. The Presidency was inclined to hand back the Social Chapter opt outs, but with pressure from the high-cost continental economies no compromise was forthcoming on keeping the European Court of Justice legally at bay. Paris agreed to the defence provisions, seeing in it an opportunity to continue its plan of driving a wedge into NATO and co-opting European colleagues into its own African military adventures. The rest was no-go, especially any reform of the budget. No, Britain would continue to have to pay handsomely for other member states to compete against it economically, while shouldering the burden of legislation sometimes specifically designed to hamstring its competitiveness.

Perhaps a settlement could have been done on these conditions decades before. But the gulf between the two sides was too monstrous, and ran at billions of pounds in subventions alone each year. With the second wind of the Recession now biting hard, this was not a season for being generous with taxpayers' money.

The die was cast. The United Kingdom could not stay within the EU on those terms.

## The Rabbit from the Hat

The next turn of events was dramatic. "Giscard emerges from Vulcania", headlined *Private Eye*. The man who had been at the heart of the European Constitution, former French President Valéry Giscard d'Estaing, emerged from quasi-retirement in the South of France to hit the Paris diplomatic scene with a conference bombshell. He had, he explained, anticipated all along about the predicament in which Britain and others would find themselves. But the project was too important to be stalled by what he saw as 'destiny's marginal players', 'wing mirrors' on the Franco-German motor of integration. *VGE* explained to the press corps that the Lisbon Treaty was itself the solution to the impasse. Specifically, he turned to a new clause (originally numbered I-56) that had received little media attention at the time;

The following new Article 7a shall be inserted:
*Article 7a*
1. The Union shall develop a special relationship with neighbouring countries, aiming to establish an area of prosperity and good neighbourliness, founded on the values of the Union and character-ised by close and peaceful relations based on cooperation.
2. For the purposes of paragraph 1, the Union may conclude specific agreements with the countries concerned. These agreements may contain recipro-cal rights and obligations as well as the possibility of undertaking activities jointly. Their implementa-tion shall be the subject of periodic consultation.

This was the Good Neighbour Clause. If the United Kingdom wanted to seek a new, mutually more advantageous deal with the European Union, then why not under these terms? If the thrust of the arrangement was one of the United Kingdom staying associated with the EU, there equally was no need to talk about whether London was leaving or renegotiat-ing, argued the member of the Académie française; it was as it were moving from one room in the 'Grand'maison de l'Europe' into another.

He explained further. Different countries already had different arrangements with the EU.

France was a full EU member.

Denmark was a full EU member with some opt outs.

Norway had an internal market association outside of the EU.

Turkey was in a customs union.

Switzerland had a symmetric free trade agreement.

South Africa had an asymmetric free trade agreement.

Georgia had a partnership and cooperation agreement.

Macedonia had a non-reciprocal trade preference agreement.

Japan had most favoured nation (MFN) treatment.

Even North Korea had 'less-than-MFN' terms.

If the United Kingdom, and possibly some other countries, did not want to be part of the core EU pushing on towards creating a common *patrie*, then so long as an arrangement was made that fitted them in somewhere away from the bottom of the list, all would be well in the house of Europe.

The sophistry was palpable, but the illusionist removed much of the vitriol from the debate in Brussels, under a baffling cloak of Gallic word play. You could be a 'member' of the EU club merely by trading and occasionally co-operating with it. More significantly, at a stroke, the French put into action their longstanding political objective of preventing Turkey from winning full membership of the EU. For Paris, the solution meant that the future status of Ankara, Kiev, Tel Aviv and Tunis, even potentially of Quebec (more Gaullist mischief, there), was settled. The centre of power of the federated European Union would not shift with populations further East, but be tethered to the Rhine.

**Associated membership** was the name given for the arrangement. The British got their deal; Free Trade and Friendship, accepting the price of a four year wind-down of the old system of contributions to the EU budget. Some were disappointed not to pull the financial support more quickly; this proved particularly acute in November 2010, when the country teetered on the edge of a national strike. Huge cuts had been required across government departments to stop the country going into bankruptcy. MPs had grudgingly agreed a token pay cut; some of the new intake had excelled in volunteering for more, though even this did not endear themselves to the GPs who were already limiting their hours in protested anticipation of a major pay slash. Nevertheless, in this context, a settlement that removed a major diplomatic distraction, while starting to return billions of pounds to the Treasury and defibrillate the economy, proved a significant and timely fillip.

So 39 years after joining the EEC, the UK rejoined the ranks of self-governing countries of the world. It was, fisheries excepted, a mostly amicable parting. In its place arose a bilateral treaty that spelled out in basic terms that advances made in freedom of movement would be kept, under safeguards; free trade would be advanced bilaterally; goods imported from third countries would not be Trojan horsed; and countries would cooperate in areas of common interest.

Parliamentarians were now extraordinarily busy. For once, the agenda was driven not by the weight of new regulations, but by Queen's Speech after Queen's Speech filled with references to bureaucratic burdens that were being repealed. A Cabinet Member was even dedicated solely to the task.

There were two further direct developments. The first was rapid. Within hours of the announcement, the United Kingdom Independence Party announced that its time had passed. Arguments still remained about the exact trading terms with Brussels and the appeal framework, but the reality was undeniable. The country was breaking away from the structure of a future United States of Europe.

"We stood, and fought, and won," declared Party supremo Nigel Farage. "We have fulfilled our mission, thanks to the determination of the ordinary members of the British public. The United Kingdom has gained its independence once again. It is time for the party to disband." So UKIP set as its wind up date the day of the formal signature of the new treaty, followed by a massive bash in a booked-out Stringfellows.

The shift of many of these ardent wet-weather political activists, once their hangovers had diminished, proved a significant factor in the messy 2014 General Election leading to the second term Cameron Government. Its commitment to "run British politics for what was right rather than for re-election" earned it short-term enemies, but gained it greater respect.

The second consequence was more of a pinball effect, or as one Italian commentator mysteriously put it, "a burning turtle". Warsaw, Prague, Tallinn, Dublin, Copenhagen and Stockholm had all now seen that there was more than one deal on offer. If they so chose, they too could seek a form of association that did not mean that they would leave as their children's legacy the loss of nationhood. For the first time in 40 years, musty consensus broke. The democratic genius flourished as new deals were struck, and a son-of-EFTA became reality.

Not everyone was happy. A number of former MEPs, who had become redundant overnight, begrudged their changed circumstance. They had ended up with a particularly generous pension, though only after a few weeks of hairy conversations with their bank managers when they discovered that, along with other Brits formerly employed in the European institutions, no government actually had any liability to pay their salaries or pensions. It was the last unfunded black hole of Britain's EU membership.

However, there were enough former EU officials in the House of Lords to pull strings and find jobs for the boys. Those peers grumbled well enough, but the number of stories that now emerged from former staffers about how the system used to be run kept most pro-Brussels heads down, and incidentally triggered some valuable reforms as member state governments forced through changes.

Come 2012, Boris Johnson's Olympics for a brief summer highlighted a Britain that had emerged from the immediate spectre of bankruptcy and was beginning to regain its confidence. The Games were not as elaborate as once anticipated – indeed, the ceremonies made a 1948-like virtue of being frugal in a time of scarcity – but the changed politics had provided a psychological uplift. The floats and fireworks looked back on the merchant adventurers and heroes of the last Elizabethan Age, but they also suggested that the same spirit would be unleashed again in the years to come.

The British had learned an unvarnished lesson from the brutal statistics of old EU membership.

The daily cost of the Olympics ran at the same level as the daily tariff of Britain's former EU membership. But the Olympics had lasted a month, not four hundred and fifty.

Thanks to such visual comparisons between white elephants, the price tag of policies such as the CAP was now abundantly clear to everyone. A question of Bread and Games, then.

# Part Three: Retrospectives

## Britain and the World Ten Years Hence

### 2020 Vision

We are standing in a fresh-mown London park. The showers have kept away for this fine cobalt day, as the crowds loiter around the marquee. Lord Teddy Taylor has just concluded his welcome speech, congratulating in particular the guests who have just received their MBEs from the King. These are honours that have been a long time coming, granted for services to political campaigning. In one case, it was awarded for over fifty years of grassroots activism dating back to the 1960s, has only now been recognised another ten years on from when Britain left the EU.

The service they rendered was fighting the argument on corners, on high streets and in markets, leafleting the public about the costs of EEC membership. At the time, most people thought of them as eccentric. In retrospect, thanklessly, they kept the flame burning.

The case has been proven by just how the EU has changed by comparison over the last decade. The Euro has pushed member states into adopting yet more tax harmonisation, and a role for the Board of the Central Bank in setting national rates.

Regions, such as Catalunya, Flanders, Northern Italy's 'Padania', and Bavaria, have used Subsidiarity to pull more financial management down from Brussels, bypassing their national capital and running it at their level. The effect is already being felt as several national governments see centralised power ebbing away. Regional governments push for more money by linking up with their counterparts in neighbouring provinces. Belgium barely now exists other than in name. Such is the alchemy of European federalism.

Defence policy has had a disastrous run in the EU. Britain's withdrawal from the emerging European arrangements had many consequences. It freed up the British defence industry from several contracts that the defence consortia would have chained it to, producing inferior products at higher prices years after the deadline (a lesson all too slowly learned from the military Airbus, Eurofighter, Eurologistics, Euromissile and Horizon Frigate projects). Withdrawal had protected Britain's special bilateral arrangements with the Americans over the transfer of technologies, and its sharing of intelligence, neither of which Washington trusted leaking out to the continental Europeans. And it woke some European capitals up to the fact that if they wanted to give Brussels some muscles to flex, they would have to pay for them.

By December 2011, the Americans had left Iraq, and a few years later, except for small numbers of trainers and special forces, Afghanistan had been vacated too, leaving the fight to a reinvigorated Afghan National Army. Yet of itself that did not leave the world a safer place.

The developing 'European fist', however, barely

lifted from its pocket. The brass buttons and brass bands of Eurocorps were not deployed during the Euphrates water dispute; the EU turned to Turkey as its proxy. An EU task force was not despatched to intervene in the South China Sea crisis over the Spratleys, since the Council of Ministers split over trade with Beijing. During the Djibouti incursion, the French were forced to act alone. More embarrassingly for European unity was when a German supplier for the Iranian Bomb was kidnapped by Mossad during a "holiday" in Eritrea. Protests by a delegation to Tel Aviv led by a Greek MEP brought the smart riposte that it had been another German armourer who had sold the Turks cannons that brought down the walls of Constantinople.

In short, the EU never had one foreign policy, and rarely less than five; but in not having five, it effectively pursued none at all.

Within the EU, integration after 2010 ran more swiftly in other areas. The reality of having a single external frontier, no internal borders, a common immigration system, an embryonic Euro-FBI, and ID cards backed up by a computer network did reduce still further the sense that travelling from Santander to Biarritz, or from Amsterdam to Cologne, you were leaving a country. The pro-gramme of training the personnel the same way, sometimes communally in 'European administrative schools', certainly made the public officials feel more as if they were part of a common European service, especially now that the uniforms are standardised. The project of building a country called Europe, which ordinary people could see all around them and to which they owed their loyalty, began to become more visible in the polls.

It was further helped by the *grands projets* that French Presidents love; big symbolic schemes that left a huge imprint, and in this case came plastered with EU flags, billboards and publicity showing that the money came out of what was now openly called the "EU federal budget". Examples included the Sicilian bridge, "spanning Scylla to Charybdis", to quote the movie advert that would so often be lampooned, the trans-Europa single rail network authority, and the new Brussels superministries.

Two of these ministries in particular drew attention for their lavish marble facades. The former DG Environment, lately renamed the European Environment Ministry, is perhaps a little ahead of itself in that it hasn't formally been given a minister in any European treaty, but then this is how Brussels has always worked. Its power is really only matched by the Office of Federal Taxation, though here again so much lies in a name, hiding a turf war between the Commission and the European Central Bank.

The Bureau of Shipping, covering the single-flagged EU merchant and fisheries fleets, comes a poor third in the grandeur scale, despite the tropical atrium. Yet it pays to look beyond the bronze iconry and unhinged abstract art when assessing other real centres of political power.

The Commission's Department of Education only exists on its letter heads. Formally speaking it remains a Directorate-General, but its role is betrayed by its reach. Two hours of every child's school week is given over to European Studies. Science lessons, for instance, explore the common ancestry of the discoverer. European language classes are compulsory, at the expense of Russian, Mandarin, Japanese and Urdu. History classes delve into the founding fathers of the EEC. Bonaparte and Caesar provide comparisons of past attempts to unite Europe. Hitler and Stalin are co-opted as reasons why the EU was created and needs to succeed. All this is reinforced by the Department's standardised school books, teaching about the successes of the European Union, from the Atlantic to the Black Sea, so that the schoolchildren of today can grow up to become the European citizens of tomorrow.

The staff naturally liaise with DG Culture, also today in 2020 a self-styled ministry. This is responsible for TV and Radio Europa, as well as an array of festivals, street parties, and proms across the EU and beyond. It is the new Jesuit Order in the EU's struggle for the citizen's allegiance and identity. It embodies the spirit of the twelve star flag, and showcases Europe's unity by co-opting its greatest composers. Beethoven, Debussy, Verdi, and the like are wrenched from time and nationhood, to emphasise the common citizenship and the mutual ancestry of the audience.

Other Directorates General are just as busy but with lower profiles. The Health people are occupied with putting together the framework for a common EU medical system. The skeleton for a common employment and social welfare system is in place, with legislation in the pipeline for a uniform welfare payment – the "first true EU tax on the paycheque". The flip side is that the red tape is again starting to flow, as bigger departments justify their importance by passing new laws to transcend borders. Sadly, the effect is a negative one, and already we are seeing a repeat of the economics of the turn of the century as businesses look to rebase themselves where costs are cheaper and interference less onerous, including, but not exclusively, Britain.

## *Le Raj*

If Washington DC was Rome on the Potomac, Brussels DC is Naples on the Charleroi Canal.

It is a fairground for lobbyists, and the world capital for pressure groups. Take the Galileo programme. Billions of Euros wasted on a satellite system that duplicated the American GPS network, and whose only function was to help Chinese missile cruisers wargame off Taiwan. That programme kept lobbyists in Dollars, Yen and Renminbi for much of the early 2010's. Then there is the constant lobbying over what counts as approved state aid, interpreted as an essential grant that keeps a social group or community going. For the past 30 years, the unofficial line has been that if it smelts, burns, types or flies, and carries the country's flag, the Commission will bend the rules to allow governments to subsidise it.

To be fair, the UK's decision to seek a new trading arrangement triggered a flurry of reform. In part, this was because many in the administration were stung by the reality; in truth, it was also a precondition of the extent of the deal struck. Over 2011–2013, a number of 'whistleblower regulations' were passed that addressed many of the concerns raised about faults within the system that had so disgraced past

Commissions – the fraud, the lies, the failed promises, the threats, and the cover ups. Time will tell if the reforms prove truly meaningful or lasting.

Sometimes the lobbyists get trumped by the mob. Back in 2012 the French had their own version of Britain's 'metric martyrs' with a group of vintners ferociously defending their vineyard traditions. A few thousand angry farmers, joined by traditional German brewers, scuppered those proposals. It certainly proved far more effective than the failed lobbying within the system that the Dutch Government resorted to during the Musandam standoff in 2015. The threat to the Gulf oil supply had led to the Union taking control of the Netherlands' North Sea reserves in order to guarantee gas supplies to member states. Public opinion was outraged, but the Lisbon Treaty articles were there for all to read, and Brussels had the power to do it. But not to Britain.

So in summary we can say this much of the current European Union; that the EU in 2020 is where it would have been in 2035 if obstructionist Britain had not left. Ever-closer Union made these changes inevitable in all things other than timing. When we visit Brussels we see poop deck territory, the superstructure of a federal state, from where instructions are piped down to the member states' civil servants below decks.

The difference is that Britain is not in the same boat.

Nor does it need to be, trading *with* without being governed *from* Brussels. The UK is a relatively populous country, with good and efficient democratic government. It has a successful economy, and respected armed forces with a world reach. As one writer bluntly put it, "If you are chaotic, impoverished and with a tin pot army you can be on every committee on the planet; you will always be an irrelevance." While not a superpower, the UK is a natural leading figure in international counsels.

Consider the UN project launched in 2011 that responded to the threat from the electromagnetic pulse from solar flares, a multi-billion dollar world crisis in the making. The danger was that a major solar storm, such as occur every few decades, would disable most of the world's electrical circuitry, taking with it water, transport, banking, navigation, policing, communications and sewage. The crisis was pre-emptively averted not by the EU acting alone, but by international cooperation on the global scene. In this the UK played a prominent part – and just in time.

## A World Player

So the UK continues to play a major role on the international scene. Meanwhile, the French UN seat more often than not is ceded to a spokesman from the European Foreign Service; diplomats from Cyprus and Malta have to report to Brussels before attending Commonwealth meetings; even the French nuclear deterrent, the *Force de Frappe*, has come under the covetous gaze of Brussels diplomats during the course of disarmament negotiations. Eurocrats, even those not trained at the European Diplomatic College but hot footing it from their offices, are swiftly taking over from EU member state delegates in international meetings. In every possible gathering place, from the WTO to the World Food Programme, from the Commission on Human Rights to the Convention on Tobacco Control, from the World Meteorological Organisation to OPEC, the trend is clear. But then, since back in 2008 and well beyond the Commission started informally calling its offices embassies, and spending €4 billion on a foreign affairs budget, it's a surprise that to anyone it's a surprise.

Meanwhile the UK reaches its own negotiating position, based on its own economic interest. It trades with EU countries; it trades with the new EFTA states; it increasingly focuses on the emerging markets rather than fearing them; it remains the largest foreign investor of holdings in the United States, still the world's biggest market. The World Trade Organization underwrites the rules throughout.

There is also the Commonwealth, for 30 years an almost forgotten resource that has started slowly to regain some real value as a political and trade tool. The recent *ad hoc* formation of a Commonwealth Brigade for peacekeeping ops suggests that there is a lot of mileage yet to be explored.

The world is truly bigger than the EU. The discovery after the North Korean coup that there had been a nuclear bomb sitting in Florida for anything up to three years sent shock waves around the world. In the absence of meaningful cooperation from a diffident and divided European Union, it was to the United Kingdom that the United States and others turned to take part in the new global alliance that resurrected the late Senator McCain's League of Democracies idea. Hollywood also profited, in a flush of apocalyptic movies based on the St Malachy prophecies after the election of Pius XIII as the new pope, but *that* is a different story.

The contrast is striking. Thanks to the absence of a strong personality at the helm, following Lord Mandelson's departure subsequent EU Trade Commissioners proved eloquently schizophrenic, as they tried to balance utterly opposing viewpoints promoting free trade while cosseting manufacturers and farmers. Yin and yang went to war. Although this generated an entertaining carnival of wordplay, it also led directly to an EU veto on the 2018 Singapore Round of the World Trade Talks. Fortunately for Britain, while European leaders squabbled and EU magnates jostled for power, outside the UK was able to enter a series of mutually profitable bilateral agreements instead.


### *Plugging the Hole*

In 2009, the EU's Common Agricultural Policy was costing the UK £10.3 billion a year in increased food prices, state aid, and paperwork.

The EU's Common Fisheries Policy was costing the UK £2.81 billion a year in wrecked communities, a trashed fleet, higher prices, ecological damage, and a surrendered resource.

VAT fraud was running away at £80 billion a year, while VAT itself was bringing penury to voluntary associations and the poorest.

Each MEP was costing taxpayers £1.8 million to supposedly monitor this mess.

But by taking the big step in 2010 and breaking the cycle, the UK in 2020 is considerably better off, with an economy that now it has regained its competitive edge is outpacing its EU competitors.

Meanwhile, the sheer amount of money saved has been astonishing.

Net payments over the whole of Britain's membership, from 1973 to 2010, ran to £81 billion. That was the amount paid in total by Britain, just in membership fees, once all the grants it had received had been subtracted.

Gross, it ran to a quarter of a trillion pounds, donated to the EU to manage on our behalf.

In the last year of EU membership, the simple net cost for Britain ran at £6.5 billion. This was the basic fee, the amount Britain didn't get back, ignoring the waste, the fraud, and any assessment of the value of the projects paid for, many of which were spurious. It was a sum that was getting bigger year on year, thanks to Tony Blair handing back, for free, a huge chunk of the old rebate.

It was only a part of the story. Yet even looking just at this part of the equation, £6.5 billion was a very large sum of money for one year.

The UK was giving more in aid to other wealthy EU countries than it was giving in total (through DFID) to the poor and destitute across the whole of the world.

If you remember all that talk of problems with military kit, that amount would have solved all the army's problems by doubling the defence procurement budget, delivering a complete fleet of Chinooks and bomb-resistant vehicles to equip and move every platoon in the front line.

It was also, perhaps appropriately, about the same amount as the total NHS budget for mental health.

£6.5 billion a year worked out as £542 million every month.

While you were away on holiday for that week in August, the country handed over another £125 million.

The Saturday you stayed over at the relatives, the country forked out £17.8 million.

While you were watching the last *Harry Potter*, £1,891,998 was transferred to Brussels.

During the England footy match, £1,113,000 left the British bank account for good.

In the time that it took you to boil an egg, £37,098 was surrendered to the EU.

£12,366 in one minute.

£206.11 in the heart pump of a second.

Another £206.11.

And then another.

It made no sense at all. It was like forming a human chain to pass gold bullion down Blackpool pier and to dump a brick off the end every hundred seconds. Every hour was a new *Angel of the North* being built by British taxpayers in another country.

The bill for just two days paid for the whole Royal Family.

Three days would have kept your local community hospital running for a year.

Five days of EU membership would have covered all the repairs needed to every cathedral in England, or paid for a new Kew Gardens.

Ten days would have bought a new Belmarsh prison.

Why not just cut out the middle man? Instead of handing over three and a half weeks of net payments, you could have simulated the financial loss by cutting down all the trees in England looked after by the Forestry Commission and ploughing salt into the soil. For the equivalent value effect of five months of fees, you could have just burned every picture and every painting in the National Gallery. Or the Treasury could have taken revenge on international bankers, and paid the annual deficit by just handing over all the revenue of the Channel Islands and the Isle of Man.

But the gain from Associated Membership was no lean figure. Trade without building a superstate gave the freedoms without most of the costs. With bold political leadership, depending on how much of the social project you thought worth keeping, the benefit ran at up to £100 billion.

The British economy could grow in such a scale it could be as if a country like Hungary had been bolted onto it. Even politicians of lesser make could have claimed a portion of that prize.

Democracy itself was nursed back to health. It set the UK and other countries free to run their own affairs, while the EU cracked on with its wild experiment at building a federal superstate which so many members of its public didn't want.

Ten years on, cutting the hidden costs, the red tape

and the burdens has allowed the economy to flourish; it created a life raft in the recession of a 2010, a spur to economic growth and a spyglass on the world.

So why on earth didn't we get round to doing it sooner?

# Epilogue
## by Frederick Forsyth, CBE

For years, the eventual destination of the EU journey has been a secret. Even reasoned enquirers have been monstered as xenophobes. But with Lisbon that destination is clear as crystal and in many quarters east of Calais triumphantly propagated. It will be, as so long suspected and denied, a true United States of Europe. The centuries-long often-tried dream of a complete constitutional, legal, political, economic and military unification of Europe into a single centrally-governed bloc is indeed the endgame and the EU is the vehicle. There simply is no alternative description after the Lisbon Treaty. All other claims are simply lies to deceive you.

So what is wrong with membership of a huge half-billion population United States that could rank as one of the world's true super powers? It is a seductive argument.

But pause, fellow-citizen. There can be no room or place inside a United States of Europe for an independent self-governing sovereign British state. The components of any United States are devolved regional territories, no matter what pompous title they accord themselves nor what local government they are allowed. Forget the parades; where lies the power to rule?

As for full-fledged absorption into the coming U.S.E. and/or citizenship of the sovereign kingdom of Great Britain, you can have one or the other, but not both. Do not kid yourself. Do not be lied to. It is one or the other but it cannot be both. They are simply mutually exclusive. So it comes to the old question of the Primary Loyalty.

What is yours? The obvious 'family' apart where does your heart lie? Where is your Primary Loyalty? EU or GB? Make your choice, make it now, and demand to be heard. Those whose real love is Brussels are working hard and fast to ensure you never get the chance to vote.

# Learn More

This book forms just one element of a broader, national campaign to discuss the future of Britain's relationship with the European Union.

Our aim is to get an unprecedented number of people talking, thinking and debating the issue – and by reading this book you've just joined in with that process.

To learn more, log on to

**www.greatEUdebate.com**

where you can:

- join the debate yourself
- watch interviews with leading figures from all sides of the issue
- get free information and campaign materials
- see our web and cinema adverts.

As you have read in this book, the EU affects more areas of your life than you might have expected. It's your money, and it's your life. This is too important to leave to politicians to decide. Join *The Great EU Debate* today!

# About the Authors

**Dr Lee Rotherham** is one of the most experienced analysts of EU issues on the British political scene. After an MPhil and PhD, a chance enquiry led to him becoming researcher for the "Westminster Group of Eight" Eurorebels during the John Major years, and subsequently an adviser to three successive Shadow Foreign Secretaries. This latter role was part based within the European Parliament.

Lee played a key role behind the scenes during the Convention on the Future of Europe, working closely with delegates from a number of countries who were united in their opposition to the European Constitution – the precursor to the Lisbon Treaty.

Since then he has co-authored the two hit *Bumper Books of Government Waste* (winning the Atlas Foundation's Sir Antony Fisher Memorial Award, Washington DC, in 2007) as well as the seminal *The Hard Sell: EU Communication Policy and the Campaign for Hearts and Minds*. Outside of politics, he has worked in such diverse areas as teaching, publishing, consultancy, counternarcotics, and heritage, and sits on the board of a youth charity. An army reservist with service in both Iraq and Afghanistan, he has been extensively published internationally.

**Trevor Kavanagh**, the author of the foreword, is associate editor of *The Sun*. For 23 years he was political editor of a newspaper that has loomed over governments, ministerial careers and general elections, not to mention plans to abolish the pound. Said to have a direct line to Rupert Murdoch, his early years were appropriately enough spent as a reporter in Sydney and Canberra. Once described by Ken Clarke as the most important man in British politics, his role was recognised in 2005, when he was the only political editor included in a "Media Hall of Fame" exhibition organised at the National Portrait Gallery.

**Frederick Forsyth**, the author of the epilogue, is a former journalist remembered for his reports of the Biafran conflict and from behind the Iron Curtain. His 1970 hit novel, *The Day of the Jackal*, marked the start of a flourishing international career as one of Britain's best known living authors. The book was subsequently turned into a major film, joined by his other best selling works *The Odessa File*, *The Fourth Protocol*, and *The Dogs of War*. He was appointed CBE in 1997.

This book was brought to you by the TaxPayers' Alliance, Britain's independent grassroots campaign for better services and lower taxes.

The TPA exposes wasteful spending of taxpayers' money at every level, in Town Halls, quangos, Whitehall, Westminster and Brussels. To join the TPA for free, please fill in the below form and send it in to:

The TaxPayers' Alliance
83 Victoria Street
London SW1H 0HW

················································ CUT HERE ················································

Title: _____    Name: _____

Address: _____

_____

Post Code: _____

Email: _____

Telephone: _____